The Executive's Guide to Navigating the Information Universe

Randolph Kahn and Eugene Stavrou

AMERICAN**BAR**ASSOCIATION
Business Law Section

Cover design by Jason Rault.

The materials contained herein represent the opinions of the authors and/or the editors, and should not be construed to be the views or opinions of the law firms or companies with whom such persons are in partnership with, associated with, or employed by, nor of the American Bar Association or the Business Law Section unless adopted pursuant to the bylaws of the Association.

Nothing contained in this book is to be considered as the rendering of legal advice for specific cases, and readers are responsible for obtaining such advice from their own legal counsel. This book is intended for educational and informational purposes only.

© 2020 American Bar Association. All rights reserved.

No part of this publication may be reproduced, stored in a retrieval system, or transmitted in any form or by any means, electronic, mechanical, photocopying, recording, or otherwise, without the prior written permission of the publisher. For permission contact the ABA Copyrights & Contracts Department, copyright@americanbar.org, or complete the online form at http://www.americanbar.org/utility/reprint.html.

Printed in the United States of America.

23 22 21 20 19   5 4 3 2 1

ISBN: 978-1-64105-581-9

Discounts are available for books ordered in bulk. Special consideration is given to state bars, CLE programs, and other bar-related organizations. Inquire at Book Publishing, ABA Publishing, American Bar Association, 321 N. Clark Street, Chicago, Illinois 60654-7598.
www.shopABA.org

Randolph Kahn: To my children, Dylan, Lily, and Teddy, who make life so much more valuable, interesting, and fun. Special thanks to the many clients and friends of Kahn Consulting for their support and business over the years.

Eugene Stavrou: To my children, Katie and Paul, who inspire me every day.

About the Authors

Randolph A. Kahn is an internationally acclaimed speaker, advisor, and award-winning author of dozens of published works including *Chucking Daisies*, *Privacy Nation*, *Information Nation Warrior*, *Information Nation: Seven Keys to Information Management Compliance*, and *E-Mail Rules*. Mr. Kahn is a two-time recipient of the Britt Literary Award. Mr. Kahn is a frequent contributor to the ABA's *Business Law Today*. Randy has taught The Law of Electronic Information at Washington University School of Law in Saint Louis, Missouri, and The Politics of Information at the University of Wisconsin-Madison.

Mr. Kahn is a recognized authority on the legal, compliance, and governance issues of information, and trusted advisor and consultant to Fortune 500 companies, governmental agencies, and court systems. As founder of Kahn Consulting, Inc., Mr. Kahn leads a team of information management, regulatory, compliance, and technology professionals who serve as consultants and advisors on information issues to major institutions around the globe. Mr. Kahn can be contacted at rkahn@KahnConsultingInc.com.

Eugene Stavrou has developed award-winning compliance software and is a respected practitioner and speaker on corporate compliance, information governance, privacy, and legal technology. Mr. Stavrou is a Certified Compliance & Ethics Professional and a Certified Information Privacy Professional.

Acknowledgments

The authors extend sincere thanks to those who generously contributed encouragement and support to help make this book possible.

Most notably we are grateful to Annette Weller Collison for her substantial input into making the book more insightful. Finally, special thanks to Richard Paszkiet and the ABA for their belief in the book and help making it happen.

Contents

About the Authors	v
Acknowledgments	vii
Introduction: Information Matters	xxi
Digital Transformation: Everything Information	xxiv
Employee-Created Electronic Information Movement	xxiv
Internet Information Movement	xxv
Communication Information Movement	xxvi
Social Network Movement	xxvi
Data Analytics Movement	xxvii
Internet of Things (IoT) Movement	xxvii
Information as a Revenue Source Movement	xxviii
Electronically Stored Information (ESI)/Discovery Movement	xxix
Why Executives Need to Act	xxix
What the Book Covers	xxx
Rule 1: Learn from Transformative Movers	1
Executive Takeaway	2
Background	2
Business Implications	4
First Things First: Assess the Value of Data Silos	4

Ensure That Employees Are Thinking about How Information Drives Business	4
Legal Implications	5
See and Balance Risk and Opportunity	5
Rule 2: Be a Transformative Mover	**7**
Executive Takeaway	7
Background	7
Executive Messaging	8
Conjuring Up Big Thoughts	8
Business Implications	9
Lead the Way	9
Incubate Information-Focused Business Initiatives	10
Investing in Information Innovation	10
Legal Implications	11
Information Innovation: Lawyers Needed	11
Innovative Lawyers for Innovative Ideas	11
Rule 3: The Days of Companies "Controlling" Their Information Are Over	**13**
Executive Takeaway	13
Background	13
Business Implications	15
Infinite Scalability	16
Faster, Better, Cheaper	16
Maybe They Are Just Better	17
Cost	17
Infinite Storage Breeds Bad Behavior	17
Generally Little Room for Negotiation	18
Do with Policy What You Couldn't Do with Contract Negotiations	18

A Lack of Control Is Being Baked into Technologies Like Blockchain	19
Information Will Always Be a Target for Criminals	20
Legal Implications	22
Lawyers Need to Negotiate Up Front	22
Legal and Compliance Obligations	22
Applying Policy to Data	23
Rule 4: Know the Building Blocks	27
Executive Takeaway	27
Background	27
Data	28
Records	28
Non-Record	29
Why This All Matters!	30
Business Implications	31
About Master Data Management	31
Legal Implications	33
Rule 5: Your Information Universe Is Chaos	35
Executive Takeaway	35
Background	35
It's a Volume Problem	35
It's a Speed Problem	36
It's a Storage Location Problem	38
It's a Lack of Organization Problem	38
It's a More Laws Problem	38
It's a "No End of Life" Problem	39
Business Implications	40
How the Chaos Impacts Your Organization	40

How Culling the Bad and Keeping the Good Can Reduce Impact	40
It Requires Guidance and Engagement	41
Build a Big Picture Plan with the Right People	41
Legal Implications	41
What Are the Legal Implications for Your Company?	41
Over-Retention of Information Must Stop	42
Proactively Address Litigation Response	42
Principle 6 of the Sedona Conference	42
Rule 6: Executives Must Create a Governance Culture to Protect Information	**45**
Executive Takeaway	45
Background	45
Making Employees Care	46
Routinized Communication	46
Policies Are Manifestations of Company Values	47
Train but Don't Over-Train	47
Audit and Monitor to Make Sure Employees Get It	48
Business Implications	48
Governance Takes a Team	48
Governance Takes Resources	48
Legal Implications	49
Lawyers Need to Participate in Building an Information Governance Culture	49
Five Qualities of an Information-Innovative Lawyer	49
Rule 7: Monetize Information	**51**
Executive Takeaway	51
Background	51

Business Implications	55
Understand Data Sources	55
Making Sure Your Data Is Clean	56
Find Opportunities to Monetize Your Information	56
Privacy vs. Money, Reputation vs. Transforming Your Business, and Other Dichotomies	60
Legal Implications	60
Anonymizing Data	61
Manage Contractual Relationships	61
Manage Trust, Privacy, and Customer Expectations	62
Rule 8: Information Changes Over Time	**65**
Executive Takeaway	65
Background	65
Business Implications	68
Legal Implications	69
Rule 9: Storage Is Not Cheap	**71**
Executive Takeaway	71
Background	71
Manage the Footprint	72
How to Attack Unneeded Information	73
Business Implications	75
Control Information Cost	75
Clean Up the Crud	76
Legal Implications	77
Rule 10: Know the Expanding Legal and Regulatory Landscape	**79**
Executive Takeaway	79

Background	79
The Expanse of Legal Requirements	80
Following the Law of the Land	81
Make Sense of Conflicting Laws	81
Business Implications	82
Lay It All on the Table	82
It Takes a Team	82
Legal Implications	82
The Letter and the Spirit of the Law	82
The Evolution of the Custodian	83
Rule 11: Bridge Worlds and Navigate Conflicts	**85**
Executive Takeaway	85
Background	85
Business Implications	89
Evaluate Information before Using It in a New Way	89
Conflicts Go beyond Official Company Records	90
Legal Implications	91
Know Your Risk Appetite	91
Conflicts between Business Needs and Law	92
The Right to Be Forgotten	92
Retention Requirements	93
Rule 12: Build and Support a Compliance Culture	**95**
Executive Takeaway	95
Background	95
What Is Compliance Methodology?	97
Components of Compliance Methodology	98
Business Implications	98
Legal Implications	99

Rule 13: Empower Your Organization to Unlock Answers   101
  Executive Takeaway   101
  Background   101
    The Tools Are Getting More Powerful   101
    Let Algorithms Do the Heavy Lifting   103
    Let the Machines Learn and Improve at Getting Your Answers   104
    Where Does the Information Come From?   104
  Business Implications   105
    Select the Right Tool   105
    Resist Shiny Objects   105
    Acquire the Expertise   106
  Legal Implications   106
    Privacy and Trust   106
    If It's Around, It's Likely Discoverable   107
    Watch Out for Bias in Algorithms   107
    Encrypt and Anonymize to Protect Privacy   108

Rule 14: Treat Privacy Like Your Company's Reputation Depends on It   109
  Executive Takeaway   109
  Background   109
    The Privacy Regulatory Landscape Is Full   109
    Is Privacy a Human Right?   109
    The United States Has Seen Privacy as a Consumer Issue   110
    But Things Are Changing   110
    Consequences for Failure Are Getting Bigger   111
    Everyone Is a Manager of Personal Information   111
  Business Implications   112
  Legal Implications   114

Rule 15: Information Security: Protect the Crown Jewels   115
  Executive Takeaway   115
  Background   115
    The Never-Ending Assault   115
    The Internet of Things (IoT)   116
    Economic Espionage as a Service   116
    The Problem of Smallness   117
    Encryption Policies Abound, Encryption Use Is Sorely Lacking   117
    How Some Business Partners Are Legally Mandating the Frustration of Your Information Security Controls   118
    Exploiting Your Relationships and Joint Ventures   119
    Manage Credentials and Bolster Security   120
    The Attacks Grow in Sophistication   121
    Finding the Cyber Hackers inside Your Environment Can Be Difficult   122
    The Weakest Link May Be Members of Your Workforce or Your Recruiter   123
  Business Implications   123
    Executives and the Board Must Be Involved   123
    Is a Data Breach Inevitable?   124
    The Need to Share to Win   125
    Perform a Risk Assessment   126
    Some Technologies Make Protecting Information Tougher   126
    Volumes Make Stealing Your Business Way Easier   126
    Encrypt Early and Often   127
    Defensibly Dispose of Outdated Information   127
  Legal Implications   127
    Think about Security at the Contract Level   127
    Think about Security at the Policy Level   128

Think about Security at the Compliance Methodology Level	129
Think about Security at the Business Process Level	129

Rule 16: Introduce Transparency into Your Information Sources — 131

- Executive Takeaway — 131
- Background — 131
  - Data Visualization — 131
  - Customer Experience — 133
  - Chatbots Are Getting More Intelligent — 134
  - Location-Based Business — 135
- Business Implications — 136
  - Transparency Culture — 136
  - Customer and Company Stickiness — 137
  - End User Interface — 137
  - Why the User Interface Matters — 137
- Legal Implications — 138
  - Companies Remain Responsible for What Their Smart Technology Does — 138
  - Policies, Laws, Rules Still Apply — 139
  - Transparency for Law Department Efficiency — 139

Rule 17: Manage the Expanding IoT Data Universe — 141

- Executive Takeaway — 141
- Background — 141
  - Where It's Hot — 142
  - But Security Remains a Major Issue — 144
- Business Implications — 144
  - Unintentional and Potentially Valuable Data — 144

Legal Implications	146
Protect Privacy	146
Laws Are Evolving to Address Connected Devices	146
Conflicting Laws	147
The E-Discovery Problem	147

Rule 18: The Rule of Yes	149
Executive Takeaway	149
Background	149
Bringing In and Keeping the Best and the Brightest	150
Enhancing Collaboration	150
Is Your Knowledge Leaving the Building?	152
Communication Technologies Help Structure Modern Work Life	152
Business Implications	153
Saying No All the Time Has Its Consequences	153
Centralized Vetting to Avoid Duplicative Purchases	154
Remove Obstacles	155
Fund and Support New Information Flows	155
Building Institutional Knowledge When Using Collaboration Technology	156
Legal Implications	156
Build Functional Legal and Compliance Requirements into New Technology	156
Protect Property Rights	156
Macro Access	157
Micro Access	157
Discovery in Collaboration and Communication Environments	157

Rule 19: Bring Your Own Device	159
Executive Takeaway	159
Background	159
Business Implications	160
Accommodating the Workforce	160
Ownership and Use	160
Security	160
Loss of Device	160
Legal Implications	162
Good Policy and Training	162
Litigation Discovery	162
BYOD Agreement with Employees	162
Rule 20: See the Challenge as Both Proactive and Reactive	163
Executive Takeaway	163
Background	163
Business Implications	164
Governance and Ownership	164
Build a Team	165
Building a Plan	165
Lean on Technology and Rely on the Village Only When You Have To	165
Be Proactive to Get Ahead of Issues	165
Acknowledge That There Are Reactive Initiatives That Must Get Done	166
Legal Implications	167
Conclusion	169

Introduction: Information Matters

A website provides aggregated housing information. And not just all the properties on the market in a particular community, but each house's value and what it would likely sell for, and a whole lot more information. The company's business model uses its powerful algorithms to provide housing valuations in return for advertising revenue. To evolve and grow its revenue, the company uses its market information mastery to develop a new market—buying and selling or renting homes on its own account. The company figures it can assess market value and seize upon attractive properties before the market has time to react. This new business model takes off thanks to machine learning.

A manufacturing company with various products in production for decades sees its future as a slow decline unless it can morph its business or pivot in some way. The company has been collecting data related to its product for years. The company lawyer and chief privacy officer cringe at the thought of exploiting the data for fear of violating agreements or even appearing to abuse the trust of its customer base. But, if they can navigate the complex maze of laws, agreements, and privacy considerations, the company could have a new blockbuster product—packaging and selling its data.

> *Noah was a small boy and very ill. Without a significant medical breakthrough, he likely would not survive. Thanks to the Genome Project, Noah's DNA was found to include a relevant gene mutation. Without the power of computing that made sense of literally billions of inputs, Noah would not be living today.*

Consider how different the world is now from when the twenty-first century began. Most of the companies transforming the business landscape didn't exist just a few years ago, while some of the oldest and most storied companies are withering or doing their best to pivot in this new competitive landscape. Change impacts the business world at an ever-increasing pace, with new technologies and new ways of doing business bombarding companies daily. And with every new technology comes new information-related business benefits, as well as legal and compliance risks and challenges. These issues have proved existential to some companies, and accretive to the bottom lines of the companies that know how to exploit them. What has become obvious is that sponsorship and guidance by the executives, directors, and officers who are tasked with managing company fiscal health are crucial. As rich as the rewards can be for seeing information as a new revenue source, a novel opportunity, or a new business direction, it is important to also see related risk and potential liability.

The winners in this new economy are harnessing knowledge and information in a different way that allows them to better plan for their business future. Other companies were unprepared and just didn't see it coming. Remember that it was not until 2010 that Blockbuster Video was overtaken by Netflix, a company it did not even see as "on the radar." Around the same time the most impressive Motorola and Blackberry mobile phones were finally being surpassed in shipments by Apple and Samsung. Note that Motorola did have smartphones and Blockbuster did have a DVD-by-mail service. But they were merely paying grudging lip service to the market; they were not listening so much as doubling down on their tried-and-true approaches.

Only two years later, Kodak, which invented the digital camera more than a quarter century earlier, succumbed to the technology it held back. And then there is Sears, the master of selling everything from A to Z (e.g., cradles, clothes, homes, tools, caskets) via its mail order catalog starting in 1893. In addition to its history as a dry goods business innovator, Sears was an online pioneer, developing the Prodigy Online system (with IBM). Around the same time that Kodak was inventing the digital camera, Sears was setting itself up in its new world's-tallest-building headquarters. Sears too has now withered away to retailing irrelevance.

We all see changes to the way service is provided and goods are selected and delivered every day now. So much so that a movie released five years ago might offer a snapshot of "how people lived back then." And before we know it, we'll be saying, "remember how people used to have to focus on the road when driving?" and "remember what a hassle it was to [insert a bad customer service memory here]."

How can you do a better job understanding what customers want now, like sharing-economy companies Airbnb and peer-to-peer lenders Prosper and Lending Club? How can you connect with your customers and engage them in ways that help you understand mood, address their future needs, and nurture loyalty, like Starbucks? Will you find the next big thing? Innovation and growth are fueled in so many ways by information. The winners in this new data-driven transformative era have a handle on their information assets: they know how to exploit them, they can readily unearth business answers from data, and they can do all that in compliance, even within a constantly growing swirl of relevant laws and regulations.

So, it's up to you to make sense of the chaos and change, and to help your organization focus on what matters. As a leader, you must ensure that "making sense" of your organization's information universe is not merely piling on more information that is valueless for business purposes or a risk and expense creator for legal purposes.

Those who master their information universe win. Mastering the information universe has both a business and a legal side. Companies that create and nurture an information culture can better predict their customers' needs, exploit markets, and conjure up new business possibilities. Similarly, companies that have their information act together are better able to protect their legal interest, comply with myriad privacy regulations, and mitigate the pain and inconvenience of discovery in the context of a lawsuit. In other words, what matters now is that information—which, for most companies, is the lifeblood that pulses through their corporate veins—allows an organization to exploit business opportunities while being mindful to mitigate risk.

Digital Transformation: Everything Information

The digital transformation impacting nearly every industry over the last few decades has been driven by waves of information technology: technology that makes more efficient and effective use of information in every facet of a business. While each subsequent wave has made business happen "faster, better, cheaper," it has also left companies, courts, and regulators to grapple with the resulting legal implications and effects. What follows is a sampling of significant transformative technologies—movements, really. Each producing information impacting business and legal realities.

Employee-Created Electronic Information Movement

The movement that democratized the use of computers gave employees the power to create and disseminate information in ways that didn't exist before. As a result of the spreading of computer use to more employees across all facets of the company's operations, a business environment spawned that, for the first time, relied upon digitally documented business activities throughout the company.

By giving every employee a computer, all employees were now free to create original company records. Ironically, the democratizing of information creation made the company's body of information less transparent than it needed to be. Employees have been generating an increasing amount of content ever since, and this trend shows no signs of abating. Some companies have addressed the risk of unfettered information growth but so many others are still grappling with the decade-over-decade growth and unseen retention of employee-created information which, at some point, may be a significant privacy or discovery liability. Courts and regulators have had to recalibrate to accept computer-generated evidence and its unique technical features, such as the ease of alteration, and what constitutes an original document.

The internet spurred a whole new volume of data that further compounded the problem.

Internet Information Movement

The internet information movement allowed companies to put information on the World Wide Web for a variety of business purposes. Employees could disseminate or access information on the company website or any other publicly available forum. The ability to move information around the world with a simple push of a button introduced significant business challenges. For example, there needed to be an adjustment of thinking on a variety of risks, such as theft of intellectual property, the posting or reviewing of inappropriate content by employees, the sharing of unauthorized data with third parties, and employees using company time and assets to perform personal activities.

The internet offered new ways for companies to advertise their products, search for new hires, and conduct a whole host of other business tasks that created various legal and privacy problems that continue to this day. Furthermore, employees accessing the web posed human resources, compliance, and legal challenges. Indeed, employee internet access created a new training challenge and a need for robust policies addressing, among other things, "dos and don'ts," where the don'ts could possibly trigger termination of employment. And marketing professionals could post product and service features and pricing on the web that also posed significant legal challenges in that the content might change often and without warning.

Communication Information Movement

The next significant movement involved the proliferation of various communications tools that allowed employees to communicate to one or many as often as they wanted. Email was one major wave within that movement that allowed employees to restructure their work-life balance based upon the availability and pervasiveness of email systems. In fact, many employees still spend a significant part of their day running their lives out of the email system. Email created great work efficiencies, but also promoted an environment of over-communication, over-distribution, and transmission of nonbusiness content, subjecting companies to binding legal obligations created via casual email. Other communications technologies like text and chat have further aided business, but they have made transacting business more casual, which has made the legal documentation of business activities more challenging. Further, communications technologies promote casual unstructured communication which traps corporate knowledge in a communication system with no easy way to repurpose it or make it available to other employees. Myriad communications technologies producing a proliferation of content has resulted in a treasure trove for plaintiffs as well as "bad evidence" unearthed from communication systems long after it should have been purged.

Electronic communications have been the focus of the ligation discovery process for years. As a result, companies have been forced to rework communications policies and discovery processes, buy new technology, and hire technical expertise just to deal with the legal fallout of the new communications technologies.

Social Network Movement

Social networks were the next big information creation change for companies. Companies found great outlets for their products and services and new ways to reach and interact with their customers in what was touted as "Web 2.0." However, companies realized quickly that they were using and relying upon some third party's technology to run their business and that they had less and less control over what employees did there or how to manage it. Social media expands a business's ability to connect with the buying public through a variety of digital connectors, such as online communities, blogs, podcasts, video and audio files, widgets and apps, crowd sourcing, and geolocation tools, to name a few.

Controlling what employees do on behalf of their companies and what customers do on social media has been and continues to be a problem for companies to address. Managing privacy, protecting company intellectual property (and the intellectual property of others), and complying with records retention requirements has posed great challenges in the age of social networks.

Data Analytics Movement

In the last couple of decades, a variety of new powerful data analytics and artificial intelligence tools have been harnessed to extract answers to business questions using existing company data. As the scale of usable information grew, human analysis became impractical and computer-based tools became an increasingly routine way to unearth answers and connect dots and transform various aspects of business. The data analytics movement is about "big data" continuing to be retained over longer periods of time so that more complex business problems can be solved, and patterns discovered through the harvesting of the information. The problem confounding big data as part of the solution is that an organization doesn't always know what information will be needed to solve a future business problem, so there may be a benefit in keeping more of it. As will be discussed more fully in Rule 9, from a legal and privacy perspective, retaining more data creates greater potential risk and cost that unnecessarily impacts the company's risk profile.

Internet of Things (IoT) Movement

We are entering the IoT movement's growth phase. There are currently billions (soon to be tens of billions) of devices connected to the internet that monitor, collect, and transmit information for a given business process and then seamlessly (and without notice) push that information to a third-party computer for collection and analysis.

IoT data is expected to grow exponentially in volume and use over the next decade. Because IoT information's creation and transmission is largely hidden from employees, its volume and use grow largely unfettered. An example of IoT data may be output generated by an energy company through a smart device that monitors and collects information to ensure a seamless flow of electricity throughout its network or to detect component part failures within its systems.

> A judge has ruled that New Hampshire authorities investigating the murders of two women can examine recordings made by an Amazon Echo speaker with the Alexa voice assistant.[1]

IoT devices create significant potential information security risks for companies in that they can sacrifice private information or intellectual property, among other things. Improper access to a device can create harm beyond the apparent scope of the device itself and its stored information. For example, improperly accessing GM's OnStar computer system or a Tesla's self-driving capability might give access to a car or an entire system to a bad actor for a nefarious intent.

Information as a Revenue Source Movement

We have entered yet another new phase, where companies now routinely package their information and sell it to third parties as a new source of revenue. The confluence of artificial intelligence technologies, IoT device data, and robotics will only further grow the potential of the Information as a Revenue Source Movement for companies in the next decade.

From a legal perspective this creates many new questions. For example, is it appropriate, legally and ethically, to sell such information? And does selling the information violate any contractual obligations or privacy rights?

---

1. *Judge Orders Amazon to Produce Echo Recordings in Double Murder Case*, CBS News (Nov. 12, 2018), https://www.cbsnews.com/news/amazon-echo-judge-orders-company-produce-alexa-recordings-double-murder-case-2018-11-12/.

Electronically Stored Information (ESI)/Discovery Movement

Along with companies' increasing reliance on computers in the early part of the century came a desire by litigants to exploit the resulting volume of unmanaged electronic information. As a result, companies found themselves substantially hamstrung in the litigation process. Electronic discovery and litigation preparedness became a greater challenge because so much information was being generated, and that onslaught of information was poorly managed, making the discovery process exceedingly expensive and burdensome. Companies found themselves in the unenviable position of either spending endless amounts of money on discovery or settling meritless claims because it made business sense. Changes to the Federal Rules of Civil Procedure in 2006, among other federal and state changes, sought to make the process fairer and more reasonable. However, large companies today have been forced to build a business unit to address the discovery of information. The discovery process within big companies has become a separate business process with designated resources and computer tools.

A company gets embroiled in a typical business lawsuit whose facts are unremarkable. As the case winds its way through the court, what is clear is that the company's legal position will suffer substantially because it failed to properly manage its information over decades. The case is remarkable in that the court admonished and penalized not only the company for its failing to manage and preserve information which impacted the litigation but also admonished its board of directors, CEO, and lawyers.

Why Executives Need to Act

Information and technology saved Noah.

The harnessing of information can truly be a life or death pursuit. And where it's not saving lives it's helping to reshape the global economy. What will become clear as you work through the Rules of this book is that the way information is managed is now directly related to a company's fiscal health and competitive advantage and it may, in fact, be a matter of its wellbeing, if not life or death. This book is written for those who run companies or advise those who run them. The only way information can make businesses "faster, better, cheaper" and legally compliant is when information initiatives get the attention, funding, and vision they need by engaged decision makers. According to the Sedona Conference, "[t]here is no generally-accepted framework, template, or methodology to help organizations make decisions about information for the benefit of the [entire] organization rather than any individual department or function."[2] This reality makes it even more critical for leadership to dictate, get behind, and fund a global strategy that works for the company.

Navigating the expanding information universe has gotten much more complex and material to a company's bottom line. All leaders of all companies need to see information as a valuable asset without which the company will fail. It will require senior business leaders to lead and coordinate their efforts with legal, compliance, privacy, and IT leaders within the company.

What the Book Covers

The Executive's Guide to Navigating the Information Universe is arranged as twenty distinct Rules that provide an overarching understanding of "everything information" impacting your company, whether or not you know it. Each Rule includes an Executive Takeaway, Background Information, and Business and Legal Implications. Each Rule is self-contained, and you can refer to one Rule as a primer for a select topic or read the book from cover to cover to get a full sense of "everything information" impacting your company.

---

2. The Sedona Conference, *Commentary on Information Governance, Second Edition*, 20 SEDONA CONF. J. 95, 110 (2019), *available at* https://thesedonaconference.org/sites/default/files/publications/Commentary%20on%20Information%20Governance_0.pdf.

Rule 1

Learn from Transformative Movers

It's rush hour in downtown Manhattan and it is raining. The likelihood of finding a taxi in the old days would not be good. An unemployed mechanic from Queens, in between looking for a job in his chosen career, has the capacity to keep busy and make a little money driving for Uber. As demand for rides goes up, as rush hour and bad weather converge, our Queens mechanic knows that the fare algorithm will reward him handsomely for working the rush hour. Uber has built its entire business on information, and that's its stock in trade in totality. The app connects rides with people who need them and allows market forces to dictate pricing and the number of drivers available to meet the demand that taxi companies can't. Uber tells you who the driver is, Uber tells you what car they are driving. Uber tells you how many rides they have done and how previous passengers rate them. Information captured and displayed in a compelling way for potential passengers makes for a more comfortable and less risky experience. Uber has transformed transportation and its technology didn't exist a few short years ago.

Executive Takeaway

Learn from organizations that have transformed their processes, businesses, and even their industries. An understanding of the power of information is increasingly the difference between thriving and falling behind.

Background

> [Former Sears CEO] Frank DeSantis: Sears was the Amazon of its day. It sold everything for everybody. The catalogue was the precursor to the internet. It gave access to everything in the store to people around the country. Over the course of 100-plus years, Sears had accumulated a wealth of customer shopping data.
>
> Sears had anticipated the changing trends so many times in the past. But it missed the biggest change in recent history, the shift to online shopping.[1]

For any company, information can be a differentiator. Even if a company has been around for decades making widgets, its information, along with its relationships, talent, and intellectual property, is as real as any physical plant or inventory. Let's get this one point out of the way before we dive in: *your* organization is an information business, even if you don't think it is.

Granted, for certain businesses, information is all there is. Airbnb, which makes nothing but connections, is one such company. It links consumers with lodging in private homes, electronically. The potential guest learns about deals via apps or alerts. Consider how the emergence of Lyft and Uber ride-hailing apps changed thinking

---

1. Suzanne Kapner, *How Sears Lost the American Shopper*, Wall Street Journal (Mar. 15, 2019), https://www.wsj.com/articles/how-sears-lost-the-american-shopper-11552647601.

about traveling. And think about how that shift in thinking has upended whole industries. Operating a yellow taxi in New York City still requires ownership of one of the 13,500 medallions from the Taxi and Limousine Commission. The price of a medallion rose as high as $1.3 million in 2013. By January 2019 it sank *nearly 90 percent.*

Newly available data, connectivity, and insight are helping shake up industries and even how companies and their customers think about how business is done in an information-intensive economy. This dynamic environment often benefits the consumer and delivers completely new service and product offerings. As a result, all businesses must pivot or perish.

Successful companies use information technology to cut through the noise caused by extraneous information that confuses rather than clarifies. Having, harnessing, and harvesting the right information can transform a business, including the administrative processes within it.

Administrative processes such as talent acquisition have been substantially enhanced by the harnessing of free and available information. Hiring today, by transformational companies, uses an approach that is completely different from the way things were done a decade ago. Access to bountiful social media tells us if a candidate is a right fit, has the necessary work ethic, or is subject to distractions that may impact his or her performance.

> Some companies are embracing technology solutions that are specifically designed to help reduce unconscious bias in the hiring process. One company, Blendoor, designed software to present candidates to companies without their name, age, photo or university information.[2]

---

2. Alexandra Dickinson, *Artificial Intelligence Brings Changes to Hiring and Negotiation*, Forbes (Aug. 3, 2017), https://www.forbes.com/sites/alexandradickinson/2017/08/03/artificial-intelligence-brings-changes-to-hiring-and-negotiation/#47a6a72e4669.

Some companies get it. They leverage the information they have and allow themselves to see their information universe clearly.

BUSINESS IMPLICATIONS

First Things First: Assess the Value of Data Silos

Leaders in every organization need to know what information the organization has and how it can be used to better their own business or be sold to increase revenue (see Rule 7 on monetization). You can't harness your information if you don't know it exists. Many companies find themselves in that reality today.

When you have hundreds or thousands or tens of thousands of employees managing different parts of your information universe on a daily basis, it can be difficult to cross-pollinate the data to find the bigger more valuable hidden asset.

Companies need to learn from other innovative companies that have pioneered new thinking on how data can transform their business. Companies need to find possible alternate purposes for the information. They also need to explore how cross-pollinated data from across their enterprise can be harvested to drive change. Leaders are best placed to foster this crucial strategic thinking.

Promote creativity! When ideas develop, enable IT, privacy, legal, and the business. Your leadership is needed to encourage the thinking that brings those ideas to life across functions.

Ensure That Employees Are Thinking about How Information Drives Business

Just because you sell widgets or services, don't fall into the trap of thinking that your information lacks value beyond its original use. Changing the mindset of the entire organization starts with provoking your employees to look outside the "information box." Each and every employee should take the time to consider how the data they manage on behalf of the company could be used to improve performance, reduce cost, impact the company's bottom line, be sold to another company that may have interest in the data, or inform future product or service development.

> Starbucks hopes to use AI to get you to buy even more coffee.
>
> Called the Digital Flywheel Program, Starbucks will implement AI technology in its popular Starbucks Rewards members' accounts, considering factors like order history, current weather conditions, time of day, whether it's a weekend or a workday, and even if it's a customer's birthday in order to make drink and food suggestions.[3]

To leverage information, those who create it, maintain it, share it, repurpose it, and destroy it, all need a clear understanding of value, opportunities, and risks across the enterprise, and not just for their own slice of information in isolation. Leaders should set the tone that is memorialized in the organization-wide information strategy. Leaders also clear the path to allow information to be used across functional areas and processes in support of the overarching strategy.

LEGAL IMPLICATIONS

See and Balance Risk and Opportunity

A clear understanding of privacy, access, use, ownership, intellectual property, and security issues must inform the analysis in order to balance risk and opportunity. Just because you can doesn't mean you should. In other words, data may be exploitable but that doesn't mean exploiting it is necessarily worth the risk or reputational damage it may cause your company. Executives need to proactively set the "information ethics and integrity" tone for the company. See Rule 12 for more in-depth discussion.

---

3. Madeleine Johnson, *Starbucks' Digital Flywheel Program Will Use Artificial Intelligence*, Nasdaq (July 31, 2017), https://www.nasdaq.com/article/starbucks-digital-flywheel-program-will-use-artificial-intelligence-cm824541.

> **Learn from the Hiccups of Transformative Movers**
>
> Facebook has undoubtedly transformed the world; the company's platform provides an array of services that connects billions of people across the globe. But today, Facebook is being reminded that although it may have the contractual "right" to exploit user data, disregarding the user's expectation of trust may negatively impact the public's perception of the company and its business.

Companies may benefit by routinizing the governance of information to ensure that an ethical information mindset pervades the enterprise. It is important that all employees know the right thing to do. Some companies are building information governance programs that seek to holistically manage information to ensure compliance with laws and contractual obligations as well as doing right by the customer. The Sedona Conference Commentary on Information Governance makes clear that "[c]ompanies, including publicly traded organizations and those in highly-regulated industries, may adopt Information Governance as a complement to their internal control systems, ethics, and integrity programs to ensure information-related legal compliance and risk management."[4]

---

4. The Sedona Conference, *Commentary on Information Governance, Second Edition*, 20 Sedona Conf. J. 95, 117 (2019), *available at* https://thesedonaconference.org/sites/default/files/publications/Commentary%20on%20Information%20Governance_0.pdf.

Rule 2

Be a Transformative Mover

EXECUTIVE TAKEAWAY

Transformative leadership sees information as a differentiator. Envisioning, nurturing, and growing an information culture requires information-focused leadership.

BACKGROUND

Executives need to create a culture that views information as valuable and a thing worth protecting and nurturing for the company's long-term growth. Employees usually see information management as a set of responsibilities and a set of tasks tacked on to their day-to-day jobs. In other words, an employee's "real job" does not typically involve information-focused activities; taking on anything in addition to their regular jobs is seen as a burden rather than an opportunity. Therefore, getting employees motivated to take on information-related tasks requires articulating an information-focused vision. This executive-driven vision must change how the company uses information, plans to make that information vision a reality, and implements it, producing action items meant to benefit the company, its customers, and the employees themselves. As an executive, you need to inspire and systematize an information culture.

Two-thirds of c-suite execs predict that global conglomerates like theirs won't even exist in ten years. Innovation will be the reason.[1]

Executive Messaging

Practically speaking, employees are more likely to follow the lead of an executive. The corporate vision, mission, and values are the "soul of the company" in that they set big-picture objectives for the organization. The vision set by executives helps guide the company. It also helps employees align their actions and projects to comport with the company's broader aims as articulated by executives. For information to become part of the fabric of your company, executives must articulate how information can and will transform the company and what employees are expected to do in the face of this transformation.

Conjuring Up Big Thoughts

Irrespective of the vehicle needed to convey the importance of a new company direction, what needs to be made clear, through vision,

> Companies of all sizes finally began realizing that competing in today's digital economy requires more than just a blueprint for the next gadget.
>
> Organizations from large enterprises to startups began seeing innovation as a platform for their growth and very survival. They began to view it as a *mindset and attitude* that must be woven into every aspect of their company culture.[2]

---

1. Alex Goryachev, *Innovation? It Needs to Be Woven into Every Aspect of Your Company's Culture*, Entrepreneur (Feb. 11, 2019), https://www.entrepreneur.com/article/327745.

2. *Id.*

mission, and values, is that information is valuable. There must be an executive-sponsored initiative to help the organization understand how information can transform the customer relationship, day-to-day operations of the company, and profitability (cost and revenue), among other things.

BUSINESS IMPLICATIONS

Lead the Way

There are likely many information-related activities already taking place in your organization. It's important to understand the depth and breadth of your information landscape. It's also important to

---

The Amazon Way

Why do industries that would not see themselves as complacent suddenly scramble when Amazon announces that it's coming? Is it simply that Amazon has deep pockets that buy market share? That's not it. And we're not just talking about increasing profitability as the result here. That's obviously part of it, but profitability alone is too narrow too; information is an essential differentiator, and it must be managed. Amazon knows that if it didn't manage its ecosystem, it would be leaving innovation, sustainable growth, and a whole lot else on the table.

Amazon started small and made things better by knowing customers and delivering services better. When Amazon comes knocking, the thought is not just "how can we compete with them on price?" This isn't Wal-Mart coming to town in 1995. Instead, it's: "How can we satisfy the customer as well as they can? They see things that we don't. They'll know our customers better than we do. Their customer experience is intuitive. They automate the tedious stuff. Customers trust them—even with their sensitive information." Think about the way Amazon minds its ecosystem. For Amazon, information is not simply something that it allows to flow through its business without thought. Information is its business.

see information as part of an ecosystem—inputs and outflows—to allow the organization to better exploit information as an asset. As an executive, you are a strategist, funder, communicator, and even a visionary. Have your organization's strategy inform the mapping of information through your organization at a high level. Fill in the gaps and gain a common understanding of your ecosystem. Focus on increasing profitability, minimizing cost, better addressing customer needs, better managing resources and money, and developing new sources of revenue. Remember, reluctantly funding incremental change won't turn into big transformative victories.

Incubate Information-Focused Business Initiatives

Innovation is not simple for most companies and it comes in various forms. Increasingly, companies see information as a way to harvest ideas that make their business better through AI and other technologies or to see information as a new revenue source (discussed later in Rule 7). Executives need to inspire and support a way of thinking that helps in developing new ideas and ways to harvest and harness company information for the betterment of the company and its bottom line. Big technology companies have business units that strategically advance new ideas and thoughts and, in the process, develop new sources of revenue and new products. Other companies should follow suit, but executives need to lead the way.

Investing in Information Innovation

Information innovation sometimes happens serendipitously. That makes for a great story, but, for the most part, innovation needs to be planned, nurtured, and funded to create an ecosystem that produces transformational change.

The reason business executives see value in master data management—if done right, a company-wide data improvement initiative—is that it allows the business to harvest company information across lines of business, improving the purchasing relationship with existing customers and revealing new customers hiding in the weeds. See Rule 4 for more on master data management.

Legal Implications

Information Innovation: Lawyers Needed

Innovative information-based ways of working can create new combinations, new interactions, and new legal risks. Every time an organization wants to exploit its information, issues of privacy, information security, information ownership, and intellectual property are implicated. Lawyers should always guide the company through new information-focused innovations to ensure the proper handling of legal, governance, and compliance issues.

> Results of an ABA survey released early this year indicated that only 10% of respondents used artificial intelligence-based tech tools for their legal work in 2018.[3]

Innovative Lawyers for Innovative Ideas

As will be discussed in Rule 18, the Rule of Yes, some lawyers are reactive and tend to look backward. Transformative information innovation requires more innovative lawyering and thinking to guide the company.

> Gone are the days when lawyers could resist technological advancements and rely solely on legal expertise. Falling behind technologically now means being surpassed by your competition.[4]

---

3. Nicholas Gaffney, *How Artificial Intelligence Is Changing Law Firms and the Law*, Law Practice Today (Apr. 12, 2019), https://www.lawpracticetoday.org/article/artificial-intelligence-changing-law-firms-law/.

4. Arup Das, *How Innovation is Becoming as Important as Good Lawyering*, Law Technology Today (Nov. 21, 2017), https://www.lawtechnologytoday.org/2017/11/innovation-becoming-important-good-lawyering/.

Rule 3

The Days of Companies "Controlling" Their Information Are Over

EXECUTIVE TAKEAWAY

Your company controls its information way less than it used to and that may be a good thing. If you're still resisting the cloud or some third-party having access or managing your information, get over it. Preemptively prepare when you can.

BACKGROUND

Most businesses today have a big chunk of their information stored in third-party environments or technology. This typically means having contractual relationships with one or more third parties that perform information services on the company's behalf. It also means that these companies store some of their information in places where ownership or control means something very different than it would have in the recent past.

In Rule 5, we discuss the expanse of your information and how you, as a leader, must be prepared to rein in the chaos and the unknowns. For at least part of your information universe, there is the reality that third parties have control of your information.

Your organization functions differently today than it did in decades past and that is likely a very good thing. Your organization may use third parties to do tasks that, while important to your business, are simply done better—more cost effectively or efficiently—

outside. Whether its outsourcing parts of the HR or IT function, or law department administration, or even storing your precious information, what's clear is that more of your information universe is being controlled, managed, or even used by folks who are not your company employees.

Where is the information physically? Where does ownership begin and end? What pieces are at risk? How do you manage the information? How do you get to the information in the event of litigation or investigation? Who has the responsibility to protect the information? The answers to these questions are not always cut and dried but they must be addressed, where possible, preemptively in negotiations and contracts (more in the Legal Implication section below). There are certain cloud providers that sell storage space with limited functionality that may or may not work for your company.

Examples: Types of Third Parties

There are many different examples of third-party information arrangements. A few are listed below.

Business Process Outsourcing: This type of third party manages a business process or activity, such as employee benefits or talent acquisitions, and includes an information component.

Cloud Storage That the Company Has a Contractual Relationship With: Cloud storage services that your company contracts with like Microsoft's Azure, Amazon's AWS (Amazon Web Services), Google Cloud, or IBM Cloud, Office 365, or Box.

Cloud Storage That Your Company Doesn't Have a Contractual Relationship With: Employees' non-sanctioned use of Cloud environments that they use to store company information.

Social Media Environments: Social media companies that provide their services for free such as Facebook or Instagram.

Software as a Service (SaaS): Cloud-based software applications that your company has contracted with. Some of these application owners may assume they have an "ownership" interest in the information separate and apart from your company's.

Third Parties That Have Evidence of Your Business Transaction: For example, blockchain technology, by its very design, is a public ledger whereby third parties who are paid to validate electronic transactions are also compensated to store the evidence of that business transaction forever in a public way.

Internet of Things (IoT): IoT devices collect data and send it to third parties for storage and analysis. This often happens without the awareness of the company using the service (see Rule 17 for further discussion).

Business Implications

Companies are losing control in predictable ways, wholly unknown ways, and in uncontrollable ways. For example, whether companies know it or not, IoT data is always automatically moved from a collection device to a storage device through the internet. Where the information resides and who has access to it is often an unknown. The increasing popularity of blockchain technology, which creates an immutable, distributed ledger, means that, in the future, companies will no longer be able to dictate how evidence of their business transactions are memorialized or tracked. In the context of business process sourcing and cloud relationships, companies need to determine what is controllable, what is not, and whether or not they can live with that reality. For example, Box or Dropbox might not provide functionality sufficient for your company to manage information in a manner that satisfies its business or regulatory needs. So, companies will either live with the risk of using the functionality provided or will need to find a different provider.

This means that going forward companies will have less control over their information and will need to find a way to make each of their vendor relationships work for them—a way of working that might not resemble the way they operate today.

> This change means that the information gathered by these suppliers will be open and accessible through technology that offers real time, end-to-end traceability from farm to table. Blockchain allows for digitized sharing of data in a secure and trusted way.[1]

Infinite Scalability

One reason the cloud and other third-party storage environments are so compelling to your IT department is that they offer infinite storage. For executives seeking to manage cost, this means having a scalable storage environment that can grow or contract quickly and cost effectively. At any time, AWS, as an example provider, is prepared for your growth, providing a way to implement hardware and software to deal with that change but minimizes the impact on your IT infrastructure plan or hiring practices. Furthermore, there may be accounting benefits to hiring a third party in place of capital investment.

Faster, Better, Cheaper

Given the growth of AWS, an environment where thousands of companies (not to mention NASA and the U.S. Department of Defense) park and process their data, there are real compelling reasons to consider using and relying upon third parties to manage your information in some fashion. Clearly, doing it "faster, better, cheaper" must be part of the calculus otherwise it wouldn't be happening.

Third parties have the ability to scale up and down in line with demand; they can increase storage quickly or increase resources. Because they specialize in an activity, they have the buying power to provide the service or product at a cheaper rate than a company that doesn't do it for a living. Third parties have basically infinite

---

1. Matt Smith, *In Wake of Romaine E. coli Scare, Walmart Deploys Blockchain to Track Leafy Greens*, Walmart, https://news.walmart.com/2018/09/24/in-wake-of-romaine-e-coli-scare-walmart-deploys-blockchain-to-track-leafy-greens.

capabilities to store data and provide services. So, you can use these third parties, but just because you can doesn't mean you should. Does it make sense to let your employees keep all their email because you have contracted with an email cloud provider that can keep adding space for email storage?

Maybe They Are Just Better

One often-articulated concern by companies, is that their hosted information (being managed by a third party) is exposed to additional information security and privacy risks. Don't worry so much. First, no organization, including the U.S. Department of Defense, is completely secure: the bad guys are incredibly capable of finding and exploiting one chink in the armor and the IT professionals have to anticipate innumerable threats. Second, cloud storage providers can't afford to have one bad information security breach because if their system is attacked all their customers' data may be vulnerable, not to mention their reputation. Third, it is what they do for a living and they are pretty good at it, and likely better at it than your team is. That being said, not all clouds are created equal and diligence is required to make sure a cloud provider's service offering fits your company's needs.

Cost

One of the compelling drivers of the cloud is usually cost. Third-party cloud providers tend to be very competitive when compared to building and managing it yourself. With storage growth happening so aggressively, relying on the cloud to manage your company's expanding information footprint may make good business sense.

Infinite Storage Breeds Bad Behavior

Companies must keep in mind that over-retention or keeping everything forever seems to be baked into the cloud storage providers' business models. In other words, when migrating into their storage environment, the cloud providers want you to migrate as much information as possible, as their business model usually rewards more storage with higher fees. Additionally, by parking more of your information with them, there is greater "stickiness" in the business relationship which makes extricating yourself that much more challenging. Some providers even charge egress fees for moving data out of their environments.

Executives should force the issue on the types and quantity of information that gets migrated to a cloud provider. Migrating to the cloud is the perfect time to address what information can be legally and properly disposed of and shouldn't be migrated. In other words, most organizations are well served to mitigate risk and expense by developing a migration plan that purges unneeded content. See Rule 9 related to defensible disposition.

Generally Little Room for Negotiation

With large cloud providers, there may be little room for negotiating specific terms into the contract. In fact, the new paradigm holds that in most situations, you enter into an agreement where you have limited ability to alter or negotiate. You buy a license or a service, and the agreement that supports it is a click of a box saying you agree, but possibly without a clear understanding of what you are agreeing to in the way of policy, ability to audit, or to get your data back.

Do with Policy What You Couldn't Do with Contract Negotiations

What you lack in the ability to dictate contract terms, you may be able to make up for in management approach and policy. You might not be able to have Google Cloud apply all of your retention policy but there are often tools and settings available to the company that allows implementation of a retention policy. Many cloud providers have information governance functionality that allows the company to customize retention rules and security rules based on content.

At the contract level, for example, you are not going to impose the responsibility to dispose of your company's data on the provider. However, most cloud providers have built in a way for you to manage your information in their technology according to your own policies and business needs.

RULE 3: THE DAYS OF COMPANIES "CONTROLLING" THEIR INFORMATION ARE OVER

A Lack of Control Is Being Baked into Technologies Like Blockchain

While the Bitcoin digital currency is the most famous use of blockchain technology, that underlying technology itself is being used to transform a wide range of processes beyond cryptocurrency management. Blockchain holds people to account and verifies transactions without using one organization as a central authority or clearinghouse—in fact, that's what makes it so powerful and useful.

The concept of a permanent, public, transparent ledger can be useful in pinpointing who owns a piece of land, what parts of a "smart contract" were executed, and how to track digital use and payment. In blockchain, those ledgers are not held by just one party. The answer to "who owns what, and what was transferred when" is in copies of the ledger in the hands of many, many parties. The power of the many is harnessed to propagate an accurate publicly viewable ledger across many distributed points. What keeps the ledgers from being tampered with? A combination of cryptography and the self-interest of the many individual users ("miners") makes hijacking the blockchain very tough. The dependability of each ledger entry can be crucial. For example, Walmart wants to use blockchain to understand the path that leafy greens take from farm to customer. Knowing that path might mean isolating, quickly and with certainty, the supplier of a product that might contribute to, say, the spread of food-borne bacteria.

In another application, JP Morgan is looking to use a blockchain-based digital coin called the JPM Coin that can

---

> Facebook's plans for its Libra cryptocurrency has the potential to transform its platform into a frictionless transaction-ready world for its 2.38 billion users. Unlike Apple's iPay, which is connected to the existing credit card systems, Libra is a new currency with the power to disrupt markets and even threaten national sovereignty—one reason regulators and central banks are taking notice. By folding payments into chat and other parts of its platform, Facebook enters territory pioneered by China's Tencent, with its WeChat app.

enable instantaneous transfer of payments between institutional accounts.[2]

Technologies similar to blockchain have a place in our future, because they may have some utility in business. But most importantly, the way companies will memorialize evidence of their business is changing, which may force you to readdress traditional information management approaches and policies.

> Cloud access security brokers have become an essential element of any cloud security strategy, helping organizations govern the use of cloud storage and protect sensitive data in the cloud. Security and risk management leaders concerned about their organizations' cloud use should investigate CASBs (Cloud Access Security Brokers).
>
> By 2022, 60% of large enterprises will use a CASB to govern some cloud services, up from less than 20% today.
>
> Through 2023, at least 99% of cloud security failures will be the customer's fault.[3]

Information Will Always Be a Target for Criminals

The cloud has and will continue to be a target for hackers and criminals as more data from more companies is located in cloud provider environments. So, while cloud provider security may be at least as good as the security companies can provide themselves, the risk of attack to the cloud is substantial given that one breach may expose huge volumes of potentially valuable information from a variety of companies as opposed to one. Practically

---

2. *J.P. Morgan Creates Digital Coin for Payments*, J. P. Morgan (Feb. 14, 2019), https://www.jpmorgan.com/global/news/digital-coin-payments.

3. Craig Lawson and Steve Riley, *Magic Quadrant for Cloud Access Security Brokers*, Gartner (Oct. 29, 2018), https://www.gartner.com/doc/reprints?id=1-5NLQ0H4&ct=181026&st=sb.

RULE 3: THE DAYS OF COMPANIES "CONTROLLING" THEIR INFORMATION ARE OVER

speaking, for services like AWS and Office 365, while the impact of such a breach would be significant, their investment in security reduces the likelihood.

> Adversis researchers have discovered that dozens of companies have leaked sensitive data as a result of misconfigured Box accounts.
>
> Box is a cloud-based "content management platform" primarily used to share files and folders and similar to AWS S3 buckets. The files can be shared to anyone with the link, restricted to those within a specified company, or to specific users.
>
> The researchers found major tech companies and corporate giants have inadvertently left their data exposed revealing hundreds of passport photos, social security and bank account numbers, as well as high-profile technology prototype and design files.
>
> In addition, they found employee lists, financial data, invoices, internal issue trackers, customer lists, archives of internal meetings, IT data, VPN configurations and network diagrams.
>
> Despite the Box enterprise accounts being set to private by default, users can share files and folders with anyone, making data publicly accessible with a single link that can be discovered by others.
>
> Anyone on the web could obtain these links and researchers were able to find more than 90 companies with publicly accessible folders by scanning for and enumerating Box accounts with lists of company names and wildcard searches.
>
> Researchers even found Box's own staff was leaking data and that some public folders were scraped and indexed by search engines, making the data more easily accessible.[4]

---

4. Robert Abel, *Dozens of High-Profile Box Accounts Found Leaking Sensitive Data*, SC Magazine (March 12, 2019), https://www.scmagazine.com/home/security-news/dozens-of-high-profile-box-accounts-found-leaking-sensitive-data/.

Legal Implications

Whether using a third party to execute a business process that you once did internally or storing your information in the cloud, these third-party relationships require upfront navigation by legal experts to proactively address issues regarding service levels, access, ownership, and disposition and application of policy, among other things.

Lawyers Need to Negotiate Up Front

Today it is common for companies to outsource their business activities, such as customer call centers or shipping logistics, to specialty companies that excel in that industry or activity. The use of outsourced business solutions has been around for decades but has recently been made easier through technology and data sharing capabilities. Ownership of information can be very complicated in these third-party relationships. When you rely upon a third party's proprietary technology to support your business process, it may become challenging to simply take back your business process when you want to. It is essential to anticipate the termination of the relationship up front because without their technology you may not be able to use your data, or even function.

When engaging with a third party that will manage an entire business process (including your information associated with the business process), contracts must clearly address issues related to ownerships, return of data at the end of the relationship, litigation response support and regulatory investigation activities, cost associated with getting additional assistance, and protection of the data. Such issues are best addressed up front, as there is likely more leverage to be had before the contract is executed.

Legal and Compliance Obligations

The legal implications from cloud use are that companies can't delegate their legal and compliance obligations. That may mean that while you may need to rely on cloud providers to help with discovery in litigation involving your company or help in responding to regulators, those obligations remain the legal responsibility of the company no matter what a contract states. Companies should not expect to delegate any legal responsibility or compliance obligations to the cloud provider.

Applying Policy to Data

Companies should not expect or even want a cloud provider to manage their information policies, which impact company information. In other words, company privacy or retention policies should be managed and applied by your company to the extent possible. This may be an issue for certain providers that uniformly apply one rule to data and don't allow for your company policy or directives to dictate how information is managed in certain circumstances. Therefore, these issues will need to be dealt with in contract or with involvement from your compliance and audit teams to ensure proper management of the information in compliance with company policy and directives.

Deeper Dive of the Cloud[5]

Public Cloud Types

Public Cloud—Individual

A well-known version of public cloud services is the "free to the public" cloud offerings, such as Google Drive. After the free storage space is used up, the provider allows the individual to purchase more. Cloud providers also offer related services for a charge. These additional services may include automatically syncing data, the ability to share content and collaboration, among other things. What this means for your

---

5. Eric Knorr, *What Is Cloud Computing? Everything You Need to Know Now*, InfoWorld (Oct. 2, 2018), https://www.infoworld.com/article/2683784/what-is-cloud-computing.html.

company is that employees can easily move and store files (including work files) that are then immediately available from anywhere. That also means company information can easily migrate away from the company without the company's knowledge.

Public Cloud—Enterprise

Public cloud services are a cloud model based on a pay-per-use basis—usually one dollar per GB—where data is stored outside of the enterprise's data center. In the public cloud services model, an organization offloads some or all of its data to a third-party cloud services provider, freeing the company from the expenses of having to purchase, manage and maintain on-premises storage, additional servers, operating systems, additional applications and personnel resources. The public cloud is by nature multi-tenanted, meaning resources are provided to multiple customers on the same infrastructure. The obvious benefit of multi-tenancy is one of reduced cost by sharing resources. The downside of multi-tenancy is that your information is co-mingled in the same physical location with other customers' information, which doesn't work for many companies.

Software as a Service (SaaS)

A software application provided through the internet via a web browser.

Infrastructure as a Service (IaaS)

Storage, database, and other computing services offered through a pay-per-use model.

Platform as a Service (PaaS)

Tools and services for developers that help accelerate software application development.

Function as a Service (FaaS)

An environment like PaaS that helps developers accelerate software development but allowing them to focus more narrowly on their own code and not the more technical underlying technologies needed to create a system.

Private Cloud Types

Internal (Within Company Datacenter)

A way to run cloud-like services for use in a company's own datacenter (not technically a cloud, considering the hardware is in the user's custody). Another form of enterprise cloud service is where cloud hardware and software are located within the enterprise's actual data center which provides the same scalability benefits of public cloud services while addressing security and performance concerns. Internal private clouds usually have higher capital and maintenance costs. One of the main advantages of internal private clouds is the control over security and privacy—the customer's data resides in its own data center and therefore under its direct control and the ability to deploy enterprise applications in a more feature-rich and secure manner.

External (Managed Cloud Service)

Another type of private cloud is where the third-party uses dedicated resources for one specific customer. For example, storage and server resources are located at the cloud provider, but are not available to other cloud customers using the same external data center. This deployment model offers the same high level of security as an on-premises internal Cloud; however, it is managed by the service provider.

Hybrid Cloud

Integrates public and private cloud.

Rule 4

Know the Building Blocks

EXECUTIVE TAKEAWAY

Executives need to have a high-level understanding of the terms "information," "data," and "records," so they can help better guide the organization, align projects, and allocate resources.

BACKGROUND

Many companies are undertaking master data management programs, bolstering e-discovery processes, simplifying records retention rules to account for technology, contemplating building an information governance program, and buying contract management software.

We'll run through more precise definitions of the terms data, records, and non-records in a bit. In a nutshell, information comprises data, records, and non-records, which can exist in any medium or storage location. For the executives or legal folks, understanding these terms can help in navigating through a complex maze of organizational activities and projects moving forward. While initiatives or projects are typically spearheaded by specific business units and employees, they likely involve *company-level information*, *data*, and *records* that affect the entire enterprise. Unless and until executives understand what each project seeks to solve and address, initiatives might not get the support and funding they need, or potential cross-functional results realized.

Note that it is also important to understand that terminology can be different from industry to industry and company to company. What follows is a list of general definitions to help demystify these concepts and help explain the various kinds of information-related projects happening in your company and how they focus on different activities.

Data

"Data" is the name generally used to describe granular, categorized content—which can be described as facts—typically stored in databases and organized and managed in a structured way. An SAP or Workday application uses a structured database whereas content in a Word document is typically unstructured.

Data can come from a variety of sources, such as transactions entered by a user or via another system, raw numbers received from other sources, or generated by a system based on employee activity.

Data is the focus of data management projects (sometimes referred to as master data management), which allow an organization to know and better handle its critical data elements across the enterprise. Data management projects allow data from different business units to standardize and cross-pollinate.

Records

"Records" memorialize business transactions and activities that have ongoing business, legal, operational, compliance, or historical value that the organization retains as evidence of its business. For example, patient files, signed contracts, personnel files, cost reports, and purchase orders would all be considered records.

Every company must retain records, which may be in paper or electronic form. There are myriad of laws and regulations that require retention of different kinds of records for different periods of time. For big businesses, a thousand or more relevant laws and regulations might dictate retention. It is also important to understand that each record has a lifecycle—a path describing its preservation, maintenance, and final disposition—the ultimate disposal or archiving of

> **How Is Records Retention Determined?**
>
> Records retention is determined by the all the laws and regulations that dictate how long various kinds of content need to be retained, melded with relevant business needs. In other words, records management is a combination of art and science that melds legal requirements and business need. If the determined business need is longer than the legal requirement, then the business need should dictate the period of retention. Retention should not be a "minimum" but rather a precise period of time, after which the records must be purged, absent a legal hold. Keep in mind, however, that employees can be pack rats and companies must dig deeper to understand the real business need.

the record. Implemented retention policies that are simple to use and comply with are essential to defensibly disposing of records.

Non-Record

It is important to understand that *not* all types of recorded business transactions and activities have ongoing business, legal, operational, compliance, or historical value. This type of recorded information can be considered a "non-record." For example, an email inviting someone to a meeting or a PowerPoint that provides employees with upcoming company events might not be considered a record.

Retention of non-records is driven by business decisions, not laws or regulations. This is important in that it allows the disposition of non-records without a legally dictated period of retention. Non-record environments can be purged uniformly after the contents are no longer needed.

There are specific initiatives that focus on managing at a data or record level. For example:

- Master data management will focus on the management of data.
- Records management projects will focus on managing records.

- Information governance initiatives seek to holistically manage information from a variety of perspectives such as privacy or security and can include projects that impact data and records. As an example, an information project that dictates retention of a privacy element contained in a record will involve both data and records.

Why This All Matters!

Different departments or functions undertake different activities that may seem similar or duplicative. In other words, managing data, records, or information may have some overlap, but for the most part, each focuses on a different way of thinking about institutional information and therefore a different way of managing it.

For example, data governance projects are completely different from projects related to information governance and records management. Data governance focuses on having a clean and accurate set of database data or data elements which allows for data to be more useful to harvest business value. Information governance on the other hand is a holistic way to manage information from a multiplicity of perspectives like records management, privacy, information security, and litigation response. Records management relates to retaining records (certain kinds of information that have ongoing legal and business value that the company needs to retain as evidence of its business activities) in accordance with various legal retention requirements and documented business needs for the records. Privacy initiatives focus on identifying and protecting personally identifiable information (PII), PHI, ePHI, PCI, etc., in accordance with laws and regulations. Security initiatives address how to protect all company information that is in transit or at rest. Each one of the separate initiatives will likely implicate the same or similar information, data, or record. For example, the privacy directive may dictate the deletion of PII after a period of time, yet the records management directive requires retention of that same record, perhaps for a longer period of time, and the security directive may mandate encryption.

BUSINESS IMPLICATIONS

Your company's rigor in defining "information," "data," and "records" will have implications throughout the enterprise in various projects that executives need to know about. That knowledge will allow executives to properly fund and support initiatives and ensure alignment with the overall vision and mission of the organization. Information is increasingly seen as a company's lifeblood, and, these projects are essential to companies being both "faster, better, cheaper" and legally compliant.

About Master Data Management

Data management projects, or master data management, allow an organization to know and better manage critical data elements. Data management projects allow different business units to cross-pollinate data in order to promote business. As the volume of data in databases grows, the importance of having a data management project or program becomes more important for business purposes. That's because such projects seek to make sure your data is clean and accurate and therefore most useful to advance the business interests of the company. For example, if an insurance company wanted to maximize its current insured business base, it may want to extract data about the insureds: their children, their ages, their addresses. If all that information is in various databases, connecting all that information to the policy number, for example, would allow the marketing business unit to know when the next generation of the policy holder may be ripe for a life policy or similar investment vehicle. Data management projects allow that to happen and much more. Because so much company information sits in databases today, executives need to ensure that information doesn't remain the province of purely technical employees who don't delve into the business value of the content. Similarly, much of the data may be considered records, and executives need to ensure that databases and their contents are managed in concert with records management policies.

Records management projects typically focus on how long to retain records. The retention rules manage the lifecycle of business information and are the only defensible way a company can clean house of unneeded business content without fear of legal consequences. Knowing the rules that apply to your records allows you to responsibly destroy them when they are no longer needed or required by law or regulation.

More recently companies have recognized the importance of records management projects that establish retention rules for non-record content and environments. For most companies much of the information it creates, receives, or manages does not rise to the level of record, which means that it can usually be disposed of immediately after it is no longer needed.

The implications of not managing the information, records, and non-records through their lifecycle necessarily increase information sprawl. If a company keeps information after it loses its business value, the company may be wasting money storing the content, searching through it to find valuable content, and increasing its privacy and security risks.

Often, records management doesn't get funding or support because it is perceived as a paper storage activity. Increasingly, the vast majority of information is in electronic form and the same records management rigor needs to be applied to electronic content that often goes unmanaged from a records management perspective. Executives can ensure that projects are translating the records management rule to the database world, for example, so that unneeded data may be disposed of properly.

Companies need to identify all their information-related projects and find a management approach that will help keep projects aligned, funded, and staffed adequately. Executives need to promote harmonization of projects and coordination of staff.

Furthermore, for all information-related projects, executives need to make sure that the proper skillsets and staffing are available as the old paper information professional will not be adequately tooled for the task. For example, records managers need to have a strong technical understanding to provide guidance on retention rules for environments, such as social media, databases, applications, third-party providers, IoT, and more depending on your company.

LEGAL IMPLICATIONS

Precision in definitions allows your company policies to specifically prescribe what information must continue to exist, be retained as a record or is otherwise relevant for preservation, litigation, and investigation. It must also take the mystery out of what can be disposed of. Furthermore, having precise definitions of records and non-records allows big chunks of non-records to be disposed of when no longer needed. Routinizing disposition through simplified retention rules augments defensible and timely disposition.

Because there are pockets of hidden information across the enterprise, having policies that proactively define what should happen with all information helps companies better manage so much content that today goes unnoticed and unmanaged. For example, popular email applications retain email messages that the user might assume were deleted permanently unless the new locations that house that deleted email are also purged. So, a deleted email may move into the trash folder for another x number of days and then it may also move into a recoverable folder for another x number of days. These settings are usually arbitrarily set by IT professionals without too much thought on how it impacts retention and litigation response for their company.

The records, data, information, and non-records definitions are not particularly helpful when dealing with what needs to get unearthed, preserved, and produced in the context of ligation or regulatory investigation. Any information that is potentially relevant may be discoverable.

Historically, litigation discovery focused on paper and physical documents, which meant that any potentially relevant *documents* would need to be produced in the context of a lawsuit. The problem with the document paradigm is that when business processes became largely computer based, most information was no longer considered documents in the traditional sense. For example, if website cache information (copies of information stored for the purpose of enhancing server performance) were relevant in a lawsuit, the document-centric mindset might have allowed for such bits and bytes to be overlooked, as they didn't resemble documents at all. With the 2006 Amendments to the Federal Rules of Civil Procedure (FRCP), what may be discoverable could include metadata (data that manages data such as a create date or modified date) or hidden data (data in trash or online recoverable locations). The legal implications are that lawyers need to understand enough of the inner workings of their storage environments and third-party relationships that may house their company information so that lawyers can properly manage the litigation response process.

The laws that deal with data, records, and information vary from state-to-state and topic-to-topic. Harmonization of the various legal requirements is required across the company. There are myriad of laws that will impact managing information. Lawyers must help identify applicable laws, navigate those laws, bake those laws into policy and practices, and negotiate conflicts between and among the conflicting legal requirements.

Rule 5

Your Information Universe Is Chaos

EXECUTIVE TAKEAWAY

Information chaos does not enhance business. It does not protect your legal interests. Chaos does not make discovery anything other than painful and expensive. Companies need to get their information under control. Taking the time to understand how your universe got chaotic will help your company gain control of your expanding information environment.

BACKGROUND

Your information chaos is directly related to a growing pile of information that has been ill-managed for decades in the following ways.

It's a Volume Problem

The information universe is expanding in truly mind-numbing ways. There is a new exabyte of data created every few hours across

> If you counted all the bits in one petabyte at one bit per second, it would take 285 million years.[2]

the globe. One exabyte of data is the equivalent of 50,000 years of continuous movies. That Mount Everest-sized pile of information is replicated many times every day and continues to grow faster and faster. It is astonishing that "90% of the world's data today has been created in the last 2 years alone."[1] The types of information companies are collecting is also growing rapidly. In the past, companies collected customer contact information. Today, they are collecting customer demographic information in volumes, including web behaviors and shopping preferences. As will be discussed shortly, this new information grab creates privacy, trust, and information security issues that the company must address to mitigate potential harm.

> The Internet of Things, connected "smart" devices that interact with each other and us while collecting all kinds of data, is exploding (from 2 billion devices in 2006 to a projected 200 billion by 2020) and is one of the primary drivers for our data vaults exploding as well.[3]

It's a Speed Problem

In the last two decades the business world has gravitated to a communications-centric business model, in which most employees rely upon communication and collaboration tools to run their business day. While the technologies promote business and efficiency, substantial institutional knowledge is trapped in unstructured data that

---

1. *Every Day Big Data Statistics—2.5 Quintillion Bytes of Data Created Daily*, VCloud News (Apr. 5, 2015), http://www.vcloudnews.com/every-day-big-data-statistics-2-5-quintillion-bytes-of-data-created-daily/.

2. Brian McKenna, *What Does a Petabyte Look Like?*, Computer Weekly (Mar. 20, 2013), https://www.computerweekly.com/feature/What-does-a-petabyte-look-like.

3. Bernard, Marr, *How Much Data Do We Create Every Day? The Mind-Blowing Stats Everyone Should Read*, Forbes (May 21, 2018), https://www.forbes.com/sites/bernardmarr/2018/05/21/how-much-data-do-we-create-every-day-the-mind-blowing-stats-everyone-should-read/#3e65942860ba.

is usually not transparent to the company. What this means practically is that your company has information that it is not able to harness or harvest efficiently. Further, because of these tools and the speed at which business happens, employees don't take the time to organize the information in a manner that promotes information sharing across the enterprise. This lack of organization regularly confounds the privacy officer, compliance professional, and the lawyer who defends their company's disorganized information ecosystem. This, in turn, can lead to bad results with customers, regulators, and courts.

In most businesses, employees are confronted with so much information that using it must be like drinking from a fire hose. According to *Harvard Business Review*, "the average professional spends 28% of the work day reading and answering email . . . For the average full-time worker in America, that amounts to a staggering 2.6 hours spent."[4] And, in any event, executives would rather have employees doing their regular business job rather than managing information.

Every Minute[5]

- 456,000 tweets are sent on Twitter.
- We send 16 million text messages.
- 156 million emails are sent.
- Venmo processes 51,892 peer-to-peer transactions.
- Uber riders take 45,788 trips.

---

4. Matt Plummer, *How to Spend Way Less Time on Email Every Day*, Harvard Business Review (Jan. 22, 2019), https://hbr.org/2019/01/how-to-spend-way-less-time-on-email-every-day.

5. Bernard, Marr, *How Much Data Do We Create Every Day? The Mind-Blowing Stats Everyone Should Read*, Forbes (May 21, 2018), https://www.forbes.com/sites/bernardmarr/2018/05/21/how-much-data-do-we-create-every-day-the-mind-blowing-stats-everyone-should-read/#3e65942860ba.

It's a Storage Location Problem

With the proliferation of applications and stored information both inside and outside the company, the management and control problem has become seriously challenging. Over the last couple of decades, in addition to companies purposefully storing their information on clouds, other third-party service providers have increasing access to or control of company information, again compounding the chaos. To put it into perspective, the cloud storage market is projected to grow at a 30 percent annual rate, taking the $25 billion cloud storage market in 2017 and growing it to $92 billion in 2022.[6] Lawyers can help address information sprawl by developing policies that dictate where records and non-records reside and also build legal and compliance functionality into contracts with any third-parties housing company information.

It's a Lack of Organization Problem

Sheer volume, speed, and proliferation of new data sources all contribute to a data accumulation environment, but current technology doesn't always promote methodical management that considers the information lifecycle and the growing number of company policies that impact information privacy, security, and retention. Traditional data silo management practices do not work in today's data growth and storage environments.

It's a More Laws Problem

The proliferation of laws and regulations impacting how companies manage information continues. Whether it is GDPR or California Consumer Privacy Act (CCPA) or any of the other thousands of laws that impact information management, what is clear is that companies are spending more and more resources trying to manage their

---

6. *$92.48 Billion Cloud Storage Market—Forecasts from 2017 to 2022—Research and Markets*, Business Wire (Jun. 14, 2017), https://www.businesswire.com/news/home/20170614005856/en/92.48-Billion-Cloud-Storage-Market---Forecasts.

information universe in compliance with a greater number of laws that at times conflict across the jurisdictions where they do business.

After addressing privacy laws, for example, legislators are now moving on to address privacy issues specific to various technology environments.[7] And when companies fail to comply, the consequences are greater both in terms of direct economic impact and harm to reputation.

> Pacific Gas & Electric Co. faced another financial hit for shoddy record-keeping Wednesday as a state hearing officer recommended a $24.3 million penalty for lapses in natural gas records leading to a March 2014 explosion that destroyed an unoccupied cottage in Carmel.[8]

It's a "No End of Life" Problem

The confluence of several factors contributed to the current reality that most businesses today are keeping everything forever. With the advent of electronic discovery, lawyers over-preserved because they thought that this was the conservative position and they didn't want to be responsible for destruction of evidence. Once information was on legal hold, it often remained on legal hold. Compounding matters, IT executives were often heard uttering that storage was cheap—a further invitation to keep everything forever. The problem is that in 2020, not being able to find information to run your business, or having it and not being able to unearth it for litigation, is only a liability. And then came big data, which likes having more data available from more places in order to answer business questions that business

---

7. *See* the National Conference of State Legislatures website (www.ncsl.org) for more information.

8. Bob Egelko, *PG&E Recommended for Huge Fine for Poor Record Keeping*, SFGates (Jun. 1, 2016), https://www.sfgate.com/bayarea/article/PG-E-recommended-for-huge-fine-for-poor-record-7958095.php.

folks may have not yet conjured up. What is known is that keeping everything forever is not reasonable or even desirable.

Business Implications

How the Chaos Impacts Your Organization

There are many business implications of mismanaging information. Employees are spending way too much time looking for information that is needed, but that they can never find. The storage budgets are growing along with the volumes, but are simply wasting company resources. Conflicts arise between your company and your business partners about who owns and who has access to information and what policies apply. Your risk increases with the volume of unnecessary information that requires protecting. The value of information is diminished because important information is comingled and clogged up with the noisy worthless information.

How Culling the Bad and Keeping the Good Can Reduce Impact

Understanding the expanse of existing information is essential in evaluating what can go away. Companies have to learn how to keep the good information and get rid of the unnecessary information based on its value. No matter which industry you are in, information is now your raw material, your business tool, and even your finished good. And sometimes, it can be your liability. Leadership and directives are needed to guide employees in taking on the challenge.

Much of that information accumulation comes from technologies that have short-term communications or collaboration value and doesn't need to be kept. But most companies are keeping all of their bad information because they don't know how to clean house without worrying about getting into trouble. In other words, IT systems are housing content (with budgets and the head count to manage it) that is of no value to the business. Worse still, much of the outdated information hanging around is likely creating privacy, information security, or litigation risk and expense. (See Rule 8 for more discussion on information value.)

It Requires Guidance and Engagement

The organization needs guidance and engagement at all levels. Executives and leaders need to provide funding and messaging related to the importance of good information management practices and to ensure that the work is delegated throughout their companies. Similarly, managers and supervisors need to ensure that executive direction is implemented across the company. Employees need to be taught to be *information mindful* and to not keep everything just in case. Executives need to create that culture throughout the organization.

Build a Big Picture Plan with the Right People

Building the big picture plan on how information will be managed requires involvement from key stakeholders in the organization. Privacy, security, legal, records management, cloud sourcing strategy owner, IT, and other roles that impact information must have a seat at the table when creating the information vision, mission, and objectives for the company. It is a balancing act to ensure that all the disparate interests are considered to address the information chaos problem in earnest. Executives need to prioritize, fund, and support information-focused activities to get the chaos under control. If that doesn't happen, then information chaos can only persist.

Legal Implications

What Are the Legal Implications for Your Company?

Greater privacy risk, greater information security risk, higher litigation response cost and inconvenience, greater likelihood of finding irrelevant and embarrassing information, undermining compliance with your records programs, and destroying evidence not in conformity with company policy or law are all real legal implications from letting your information universe swirl uncontrollably.

Over-Retention of Information Must Stop

In the world of information, more is not always merrier and in fact there is a point of diminishing returns. Having information but not being able to readily access it fails to protect your legal rights or obligations. Having volumes of information that are not needed increases privacy and security risks and increases litigation expense.

Four Ways to Make the Pile Smaller

✓ Simplify retention rules so that they can be applied to records more easily
✓ Apply universal retention periods to all non-records
✓ Apply universal retention rules to specific environments
✓ Automate the application of retention rules to records
✓ Automate disposition of records and non-records

Proactively Address Litigation Response

Proactively addressing litigation response, keeping in mind your cloud footprint and the volume of other information in the care, custody, and control of third parties, is essential to mitigating risk and unnecessary expense. Reducing the chaos will lessen the discovery burden on your company. Addressing information sprawl and chaos helps lawyers more confidentially address litigation response proactively and mitigate cost and expense up front.

Principle 6 of the Sedona Conference

Commentary on Information Governance by the Sedona Conference[9] provides the following guidance to organizations:

---

9. The Sedona Conference, *Commentary on Information Governance, Second Edition*, 20 SEDONA CONF. J. 95 (2019), *available at* https://thesedonaconference.org/sites/default/files/publications/Commentary%20on%20Information%20Governance_0.pdf.

The effective, timely, and consistent disposal of physical and electronic information that no longer needs to be retained should be a core component of any Information Governance program.

The Comment to Principle 6 explains:

It is a sound strategic objective of a corporate organization to dispose of information no longer required for compliance, legal hold purposes, or in the ordinary course of business. If there is no legal retention obligation, information should be disposed as soon as the cost and risk of retaining the information is outweighed by the likely business value of retaining the information. Typically, the business value decreases and the cost and risk increase as information ages.

Rule 6

Executives Must Create a Governance Culture to Protect Information

EXECUTIVE TAKEAWAY

Creating a culture that inculcates all employees with an information mindfulness demands leadership. Getting support and buy-in from the workforce to better deal with information security, privacy, economic espionage, and records management takes executives that make such initiatives a priority.

BACKGROUND

There is an all-out assault on companies' information troves across the globe. Malicious attacks target most big companies with an unending barrage of malicious code 24/7. Some nefarious actors may be merely up to mischief for kicks, but most attacks on the IT infrastructure of most companies are about big business. Sophisticated criminal rings see information as a valuable asset to be sold, traded, or bartered away. Indeed, countries and even military units target company information as a source of strategic advantage and attack it regularly. Theft and resale of credit card and related personal information about customers or employees costs customers and companies tens of billions of dollars annually. If it's valuable to someone else, it should be very valuable to your company and worthy of serious precautions. The company's reputation and business may depend upon it. That means taking appropriate proactive precautions to mitigate the risk and minimize the liability. It also means creating a governance culture to increase the chances of minimizing the risk and harm. Staying ahead of information security risk takes vigilance.

Developing a culture of information governance mindfulness requires actions of various kinds, all of which need input from privacy, compliance, records management, legal, information security, data governance, and business units on most issues. The governance culture cannot stymie growth and innovation, but it must see itself as part of the strategy to make the company "faster, better, cheaper" and legally compliant.

Making Employees Care

Making employees care about protecting company information is a major challenge. First, operationalizing governance of information is tough because it requires making it part of the corporate culture. Second, there has been an increase in the number of information issues requiring greater governance which usually means that there are more company directives for employees to learn and follow. And finally, winning at better governance of information requires vigilance over time. Protecting against a spear-phishing attack today but opening an email with a pernicious malicious code attached to it tomorrow means that the company may have its network compromised tomorrow and today's efforts are valueless. Getting governance right requires changing a culture, and that is no easy task. Protecting the company information "crown jewels" requires an ongoing and unending process of policy, communication, training, auditing, enforcement . . . repeat.

Routinized Communication

Plan out regular communications transmitted through an effective mix of channels in order to increase the likelihood that employees will get the message and take action. Some of the messaging should come from the executives while other more tactical messages can come from managers. Get the right messages in front of employees periodically to help inculcate the workforce with the sense that awareness of information is an important part of their jobs. Creating a culture that protects information for privacy or information security purposes, for example, also requires executive communication and support.

Policies Are Manifestations of Company Values

A policy on its own, no matter how comprehensive and clear, is only as good as the training and change management that accompanies it. Parking a library of policies on an intranet site and thinking employees will search to find and master them is unrealistic. And having policies that no one follows is a liability. "Isn't it true that your company has a privacy policy that you didn't know about and that you, in fact, were never trained on?" You get the idea.

Providing a written policy or other directive tells employees what is expected, training them on it helps ensure they understand what they need to do specifically. But policy alone is not enough. Training and perhaps even testing on the mastery of the content is far more effective.

Train but Don't Over-Train

Remember, employees can't take in endless training on countless topics. So, be mindful to not put too much in front of them and spread

---

What Is Gamification and Can It Help?

Gamification is the process of applying game-playing techniques to other activities to encourage better engagement and behavior. It can be used and has been used in the company context by gamifying various types of training to make it a bit more memorable and fun by involving levels of mastery, points, or awards. Because having employees master information security training can be hard and boring, gamification can help make the training material more understandable and actionable. Gamification engages employees so that they want to revisit the training material and that promotes mastery.

it out, coordinating across the various functions that also need to get their message across, to maximize effectiveness. Be sure to limit how much training employees get to avoid the point of diminishing returns. Make the topic a formal job responsibility if the company wants employees to do it. Putting responsibilities in writing tends to elevate their importance and can make clear that failure to do as required will impact the employee.

Audit and Monitor to Make Sure Employees Get It

To ensure that employees are getting it right, the company should have an ongoing program to audit and monitor actions and conduct. It's not enough to tell employees what to do. Management must fund and support a periodic review of employees' actions to make sure they understand their responsibilities and are doing what is required. Executives can help create a governance and compliance culture (compliance methodology is addressed in Rule 12).

Business Implications

Governance Takes a Team

Getting governance right takes a team. Chief privacy officers think about protecting privacy, but that can't be accomplished without the help of CIOs or CTOs, who own the technology and infrastructure. Policies can be drafted by lawyers, but training professionals will need to develop simple and brief training modules that keep the interest of employees. That interest increases the likelihood that they will understand what is needed and do it. In other words, it takes the involvement of a range of people, each with a slightly different purview, each of which contributes to addressing the issue holistically.

Governance Takes Resources

Every dollar spent on protecting resources is viewed as a cost. Every employee not focusing on the company's core business is seen as not building profit. That said, company reputation is inextricably linked to trust: protecting customer data, for example. So, executives need to ensure that information governance initiatives get the resources and funding to make them successful.

Legal Implications

Lawyers Need to Participate in Building an Information Governance Culture

Increasingly, courts and regulators are expecting more from companies in the way they manage information and they are seemingly more likely to impose culture changes upon the company's information management regime when it fails. For example, in the Premera data breach case, which impacted the data of millions of patients, the settlement included compensation to the breach victims but also a greater amount of money—nearly $42 million—to fix IT security and information management at the company.[1] When companies fail, courts and regulators are increasingly willing to impose a greater information culture change on companies than in the past. Companies are well served to take on these issues preemptively as not doing so can be more expensive and painful.

Five Qualities of an Information-Innovative Lawyer

The information landscape creates new opportunities for legal professionals to guide on the governance, risk, and legal issues of information and to help the company innovate, grow, and evolve.

---

1. Jessica Davis, *Premera Reaches Proposed $74M Settlement Over 2014 Breach of 11M*, Health IT Security (Jun. 4, 2019), https://healthitsecurity.com/news/premera-reaches-proposed-74m-settlement-over-2014-breach-of-11m?eid=CXTEL000000460483&elqCampaignId=10035&elqTrackId=d9f542ab981e4c6d8acdcfc957a6ce9a&elq=2fb4af2e83714ef795027005477f7ae9&elqaid=10542&elqat=1&elqCampaignId=10035.

An information-innovative lawyer needs to be the following at a minimum:

1. Technology aware: the lawyer should understand technology and not be fearful of learning new technology.
2. Technically conversant: the lawyer should be able to communicate with technology and information professionals, understanding their language, concerns, and business drivers.
3. Bottom line aware: the lawyer should understand how information initiatives and information failures impact the bottom line—the law department cannot function in a vacuum.
4. Solution creator: the lawyer must find ways to bring about business change for the betterment of the company while also protecting legal interests.
5. A good team member: in order to maximize information as a business, the lawyer needs to see his or herself as a member of a larger business team and needs to creatively develop risk-adjusted business solutions.

Rule 7

Monetize Information

EXECUTIVE TAKEAWAY

Your information is valuable to your company, and maybe to others, so manage it as an asset. It's your job to protect and properly utilize your information assets as you would traditional corporate assets.

BACKGROUND

> The table-booking service will block restaurants from giving competitors access to diner data acquired through OpenTable unless they pay new fees, according to its updated client agreement.[1]

Companies nurture and support employees. Companies insure their buildings and make sure their infrastructure is up to date and secured. Their stock in trade is also managed to protect their business interests and maximize profitability. For most businesses, even in 2020, the same cannot be said for the way they manage information.

There is no shortage of public pronouncements on just how valuable information is. You hear them all the time and they are no

---

1. Micah Maidenberg, *Who Controls Diners' Data? OpenTable Moves to Assert Control*, Wall Street Journal (Mar. 15, 2019), https://www.wsj.com/articles/who-controls-diners-data-opentable-moves-to-assert-control-11552644121.

doubt true to a certain degree. "We live in an information economy." "Information is the lifeblood of our organization."

Information can help you know your customer better, understand which products to build to address future demand, design more effective tools, better manage and reduce risk, reduce costs in running your business, maximize the use of employee time, manage costs associated with the use of outside consultants, and improve productivity, among other things. All this begs the question, given contractual obligations, privacy, and customer trust, in what ways can your company's information be valuable? And how valuable?

> In the information space, having information is very different than managing it, and most companies are not managing information effectively in large part because the rules they use are no longer ready for prime time.[2]

There are myriad ways to use, aggregate, exploit, package, distribute, barter, utilize, or otherwise monetize information. In fact, your organization is harnessing various facets of its information's value every day to run its business.

> Unlike most of your enterprise's other assets, information isn't depleted after it's consumed.[3]

Let's say some information was collected initially to support a specific business process such as customer service, procurement, or quality. It now may have a secondary use to the organization or other organizations. So, customer preference data can be used to predict future resource needs but also can be exploited by selling it to a third party.

---

2. Randolph Kahn, *The Incredibly Compelling Case to Rethink Records Retention in 2018 and Beyond*, Business Law Today (Feb. 12, 2018), https://businesslawtoday.org/2018/02/the-incredibly-compelling-case-to-rethink-records-retention-in-2018-and-beyond/.

> A large number of monetization opportunities are created using actionable customer insights from big data, especially in the consumer packaged goods and retail sectors. Through its Retail Link trading partner portal, Walmart gives suppliers its entire sell-through data—almost in real time, and by store. Companies create additional services based on the customer data they collect. For example, Alibaba offers targeted personal finance products to customers that are active on its digital commerce sites.[4]

A medical device manufacturer, for example, has completely retooled its business model over the past couple of decades in two distinct steps. First, the global company made a conscious move from dumb products, those with no computing power, to smart

> For a long time, the data economy seemed fairly benign. It was less obtrusive than, say, telemarketing, but nonetheless personalized the internet experience to be of maximum benefit to its users. The tradeoff between users and companies also seemed fair. Instead of shelling out for pricey software packages, users got access to "free" services, while companies rewarded with a well of information worth far more than a simple one-off payment.[5]

---

3. Heather Levy, *Are You Getting the Most Value Out of Your Organization's Information? Uncover the Probable and Potential Value*, Gartner (Jun. 7, 2016), https://www.gartner.com/smarterwithgartner/three-degrees-of-information-value/.

4. Susan Moore, *Customer Data Is a Key Component of Customer Relationship Management (CRM), but Does Your Business Recognize and Leverage Its Real Value?*, Gartner (Dec. 10, 2015), https://www.gartner.com/smarterwithgartner/how-to-monetize-your-customer-data/.

5. Luke Dormehl, *Yes, Data Is the New Oil and the Fight to Reclaim It from Tech Giants Starts Now*, Digital Trends (Mar. 2, 2019), https://www.digitaltrends.com/cool-tech/2019-year-fight-back-data-grubbers/.

products. What makes them smart is computing or data aggregation functionality that monitors and collects information about the use of the company's meters and monitoring devices. The devices are inserted into patients to regulate various organs and processes. That same company now realizes that all that data collected and aggregated from its smart devices offer great business utility to medical providers, insurance companies, and other businesses. Their new business—assuming they continue to address the complex privacy and information ownership questions—is the aggregation and sale of the various databases they now generate from devices in patients' bodies, and automatically sent back to the company for analysis and use for the company's internal purposes. According to the general counsel the company will be mining and selling its data in the near future, but she has to figure how to make it work given existing contracts and privacy issues and, of course, the public trust. In other words, they aim to exploit their information universe in new ways with new potential for revenue. Why is their packaged information valuable? In their case, it can help create better tailored solutions and care, reduce the cost of care, and perhaps provide greater comfort and even save lives. It might even present patterns used to unearth new medical issues before they would otherwise be diagnosed.

> From gateways to issuers, today's payments providers have a treasure trove of data at their fingertips. By using it to generate insights into consumer purchasing behavior, and coupling these insights with an understanding of emerging macro trends, payments firms can provide better service to customers—from fraud detection to spending insights.[6]

---

6. Alessio Botta, Nunzio Digiacomo, and Kevin Mole, *Monetizing Data: A New Source of Value in Payments*, McKinsey (Sep. 2017), https://www.mckinsey.com/industries/financial-services/our-insights/monetizing-data-a-new-source-of-value-in-payments.

Business Implications

Understand Data Sources

Knowing your company information sources includes information within the company, your information at third parties with whom you contract, and possibly a mashup of information (an aggregation of different information sources, some of which may not be yours). Knowing what information you have better allows you to figure out how to share, harness, and harvest information in your company across lines of business and outside the company. Knowing your sources of information is only the beginning of the inquiry. You also need to understand the type of information included.

Information is generally split into two categories: *structured* and *unstructured*. Structured data is stored in an organized database, where elements of data are labeled and relationships between elements might be charted. Today, this accounts for much of the information in a company and it is relatively easy to analyze (e.g., SAP and Oracle systems leverage relational databases to store their data). Structured data is usually administered by IT or maybe a third-party cloud provider, but either way, its structured nature helps in its use and exploitation. But we will come back to that concept shortly. Unstructured data is not organized in a pre-defined manner and it is usually managed by the average employee (e.g., the content stored in a Word document or PowerPoint presentation stored on a personal or shared drive). This data is more difficult to identify and manage in aggregate. Both types of information may have value, but structured data is easier to harvest for business purposes because of the way it is organized. As discussed in Rule 5, applying better management rigor to unstructured data will make it more usable to your company.

For lawyers, compliance, and privacy professionals, the idea of selling data may not smell right or sit well because of the risk and downside to reputation and the violation of contractual obligations and privacy regulations. This is where business and legal folks need to work together to ensure that information monetization can be done prudently.

Making Sure Your Data Is Clean

Cleaning your data is the process of making sure that the company has accurate and up to date information in its databases. Many organizations are taking on initiatives called master data management (MDM) or data management which allows the company to establish a set of information that is correct, accurate, and time relevant—allowing them to cross-pollinate across their company and across other lines of business more easily. Critical data elements are essential common data categories used across the company that can include product code, customer number, claim number, and much more. Big companies will have thousands of data elements that appear in various kinds of databases. Investing in building a list of critical data elements allows the company to determine which data elements are essential to run their business and facilitates the understanding of their information across lines of businesses. This harvesting can promote new sales, spur product development, and help anticipate customer needs, for example.

In the context of unstructured environments, having policies that direct what information can reside in certain environments and systemically purging content that is not valuable for long-term business purposes is essential. Further, as we will discuss in Rule 13, applying analytics and AI tools can assist in unearthing value in the unstructured environments.

Making sure the data is clean and of high quality becomes essential to harvesting the data for business purposes.

Find Opportunities to Monetize Your Information

To jumpstart your efforts to monetize information, understand and evaluate what other companies are doing—even those outside your own industry. Looking at successes beyond your industry is important. You can get good ideas from them, but you can also get ahead of how other companies, perhaps in industries with a more impressive technology track record, are evolving their information monetization initiatives. New ideas, inspiration, and new thinking about how to use your data can be found in public case studies, professional organizations, and industry conferences.

> Some of the largest lenders in the U.S. are now sharing their loan-approval process with consumer finance app Credit Karma.
>
> This unprecedented move comes as lenders struggle amid high competition, rising interest rates and fewer borrowers.[7]

> This ever-growing compilation includes hundreds of stories from every sector, every geography, and the majority of business domains and information types, including:
>
> - How Lockheed-Martin text mines project documentation and communications for leading indicators of project issues, leading to hundreds of millions of dollars in reduced cost overruns.
> - How Walmart reduced online shopping cart abandonment by 10–15 percent by incorporating social media trends into its search scoring algorithm.
> - How Minute Maid can replan its orange juice blending operation in just minutes using a bevy of external information sources.
> - How the Mexican oil company Pemex used a fleet of sensors to shift from unplanned to planned maintenance, saving hundreds of hours of oil refinery downtime.
> - How DBS Bank in Singapore saves 30,000 hours of customer wait time by optimizing its replenishment of ATMs.
> - How Primary Capital Mortgage has reduced the time loan officers spend tracking loan status from 1–2 hours to under five minutes per day, saving $10M annually.
> - How the Georgia Aquarium used data science to turn a $700,000 media spend into a $8M of incremental revenue.

---

7. Kelsey Ramirez, *Lenders Reveal Their Secret Sauce to Credit Karma*, Housingwire (Oct. 23, 2018), https://www.housingwire.com/articles/47203-lenders-reveal-their-secret-sauce-to-credit-karma.

- How Dollar General has a self-funding data warehouse by licensing its data to suppliers.
- How CVS Health reduced call center resolution time by a minute per call by intelligently matching callers and CSRs.
- How the Peruvian insurer RIMAC used artificial intelligence to process claims 25 times faster than it once did.[8]

Companies are monetizing information in ways that are truly transforming industries and/or behavior.

Over 200 data points exist today, typically providing more than 140 viable use cases, but only 15% of these use cases are being monetized. Though use cases can be grouped under usage-based insurance (UBI), autonomous vehicles (AVs), crash reconstruction, location and mapping services, there are several kinds of uncharted potential. Use cases using location, driver behavior and vehicle use data (e.g. real-time location-based promotions, ride sharing specific insurance, digital car maintenance books) could find immediate monetization opportunities for the time spent in the car as an immediate ROI.[9]

---

8. Doug Laney, *Monetizing and Innovating with Information: The Art of the Possible*, Gartner Blog Network (Nov. 5, 2017), https://blogs.gartner.com/doug-laney/monetizing-innovating-information-art-possible/.

9. Sarwant Singh, *Are Car Companies Going to Profit from Your Driving Data?*, Forbes (Nov. 6, 2017), https://www.forbes.com/sites/sarwantsingh/2017/11/06/are-car-companies-going-to-profit-from-your-driving-data/#4ae1ec4143c8.

> ### WSJ "Open Your App and 'Say Ahh'"[10]
>
> Smartphones and better health records have the potential to revolutionize medicine.
>
> The data collected by a new generation of digital health products—including smart watches, smartphones, and fitness trackers—could help the medical community learn about treatments that might work for a patient like you, and which ones to avoid. The first is enabling them to stream data wirelessly to your doctor's EHR.

Unintended information creation from a growing number of IoT devices in use at most big businesses is something that your organization will have to deal with over the coming years. But more than that it will need to rethink the security around IoT devices. Unlike smartphones or personal computers, the internet-connected things inside factories, home and cities aren't generally protected with anti-virus software and users often aren't asked to update logins and password. That makes access to these things—which now number more than 10 billion globally, according to market researcher Gartner Inc.—easier to cloak malware, mask data thefts or gain remote access control.[11]

---

10. Sean Khozin and Paul Howard, *Open Your App and Say "Ahh,"* Wall Street Journal (Sep. 19, 2018), https://www.wsj.com/articles/open-your-app-and-say-ahh-1537397802.

11. Timothy W. Martin, *New Cyberdefenses to Protect Your Smart Appliances From Hackers*, Wall Street Journal (Oct. 18, 2018), https://www.wsj.com/articles/the-hackers-at-your-smart-door-new-cyberdefenses-planned-for-connected-devices-1539770321.

Privacy vs. Money, Reputation vs. Transforming Your Business, and Other Dichotomies

As we will explore in Rule 11, oftentimes information use creates conflicts between competing interests within the organization, and it's the executive's task to properly navigate those conflicts. Is the business running afoul of the law or regulation by selling or sharing information with a partner? Does the act of monetizing a customer's information violate a contractual obligation? Even if there are no legal ramifications from selling information, will customers perceive the sale as a violation of trust? Striking a balance between protecting the customer and monetizing the data is an essential task and one in which the lawyers need to be involved.

> Facebook just got its first penalty after the Cambridge Analytica scandal broke. The UK's Information Commissioner's Office (ICO) has fined the social network a preliminary amount of £500,000 or $664,000 (maximum allowed by the law), saying that the company lacked proper privacy protection and failed to catch warning signs that Cambridge Analytica was abusing users' data.
>
> The ICO essentially blamed Facebook for the scandal, saying that it let researcher Aleksandr Kogan gather user data via an app and didn't warn its users when discovered. The commission also found a "shortfall in transparency" from tech firms and their third-party companies, which are involved in collecting and selling users' data.[12]

LEGAL IMPLICATIONS

As discussed above, selling, bartering, or exchanging data with anyone has well-publicized potential risk associated with it. Here are things to consider when addressing these challenges.

---

12. Selene Kyle, *Facebook Penalized over Cambridge Analytica Scandal*, TechWorld (July 11, 2018), http://thetechnews.com/2018/07/11/facebook-penalized-over-cambridge-analytica-scandal/.

> **WSJ "What Your Car Knows About You"**
>
> Car makers are collecting massive amounts of data from the latest cars on the road. Now they're figuring out how to make money off of it.[13]

Anonymizing Data

There is a tradeoff to be made between privacy and accuracy. While there may be precise data available that allows you to tailor ads or services directly to a customer, using the data may be non-compliant if, say, the customer has handed over the information but has not consented to a particular use. And if it is acceptable to use, it still might not pass the smell test and it might appear to pose a breach of trust.

One of the ways to address the complexities of privacy and trust is anonymizing the data so that it can't be directly related to a specific person, so it can be sold without breaching a contract or the customers' trust. Anonymizing essentially rids the data of personally identifiable information that would link the data to an individual.

Again, it is useful to have lawyers directly involved in the business decisions to monetize information in order to ensure that laws and regulations are not violated.

Manage Contractual Relationships

Before doing anything with information that may breach an express or implied contractual obligation, lawyers need to both review the legal obligations with customers and clients, and assess the obligations and limitations related to sharing and selling information with third parties. There may be contracts with customers that may be different from contracts with third parties, and all that needs to be considered.

---

13. Christina Rogers, *What Your Car Knows About You*, Wall Street Journal (Aug. 18, 2018), https://www.wsj.com/articles/what-your-car-knows-about-you-1534564861.

Manage Trust, Privacy, and Customer Expectations

While the instinct of some companies may be to grab as much customer information as possible and protect themselves with dense legalese, this approach will increasingly be called out by the public opinion, regulators, and the courts.

When it comes to customer or client consent in the context of using their data, companies need to be overly protective of their rights. So, companies should not play fast and loose with processes that technically capture consent where the customer doesn't actually understand or agree to let their data be used. For example, requiring click throughs with complex legalese is likely not going to pass the smell test and complex and multiple screen opt-out provisions that don't really explain what customers or clients are doing should not be used in this environment. Using a website to put customers through hoop-jumping exercises is not prudent. It is best to err on the side of over-sensitivity and over-compliance when it comes to company obligations to customers. Requiring that a user opt-in is preferable than expecting them to opt-out, and increasingly, it is the law.

Google Hit With $57M Fine Under New EU Law Over Targeted Ads[14]

France's data privacy watchdog fined Google €50 million ($57 million) on [January 21, 2019], the first penalty for a U.S. tech giant under new European data privacy rules that took effect last year.

---

14. *Google Hit With $57M Fine Under New EU Law Over Targeted Ads*, HuffPost (Jan. 21, 2019), https://www.huffingtonpost.com/entry/google-hit-with-57m-fine-under-new-eu-law-over-targeted-ads_us_5c460e4de4b027c3bbc45de6.

The National Data Protection Commission said it fined the U.S. internet giant for "lack of transparency, inadequate information and lack of valid consent" regarding ad personalization for users.

The commission said Google users were "not sufficiently informed" about what they were agreeing to as the company collected data for targeted advertisements.

Users have to take too many steps, "sometimes up to 5 or 6 actions," to find out how and why their data is being used, the commission said. Google's description of why it's processing their data is "described in a too generic and vague manner," it added.

The company's infringements "deprive the users of essential guarantees regarding processing operations that can reveal important parts of their private life," the commission said.

Rule 8

Information Changes Over Time

Executive Takeaway

Understand that information has a lifecycle and that its value changes over time. Recognizing this variable value will help your organization maximize utility and minimize risk.

Background

Information does not come into existence with a set value. Value is typically dictated by the utility of the content to the organization, and that utility is time-limited in some way. Most information's value goes down precipitously after a short period of time. However, today most organizations retain information seemingly forever because they either don't know how to get rid of it in a legally defensible way or they think that it has value forever. Or they think "storage is cheap" so why not just keep it. Importantly, however, while the cost of managing information over time might remain a constant, risk may rise.

An employee's request for vacation time is relevant in the short-term to ensure that the employee is in compliance with the time off policy and is appropriately compensated, but that information's value drops off rather rapidly. Similarly, a business unit's budget planning information has great relevance in the near term but limited utility down the road. M&A targets are relevant currently but

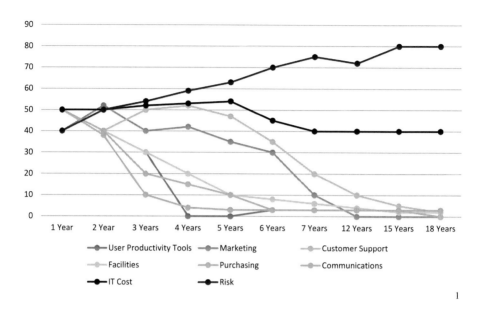

[1]

have no value a short while after the deal is dead. We can quibble about exactly how long information should stick around but the fact remains that none of this information should exist forever as there is limited value and only cost and risk associated with it. And, that brings us to the discussion of lifecycle.

The analysis of weighing all the laws relevant to business interests for how long information should be retained is really the art and science behind record retention.

So, when is information considered valuable to your organization and when is it a risk? To answer this question, it is helpful to understand that all information in your organization has a lifecycle. It is created or received, used more or less often by the employees depending upon where they sit and what they do, it is maintained for

---

1. The graph displays how the value of the information types used in your organization change over time. While the graph is provided for illustration purposes only, it makes the point that the value of information goes down over time while risk of retaining that information goes up over time. (Graph created by the authors from information provided by IBM's CGOC group.)

a stretch of time, and then it reaches final disposition (when it must be archived or deleted). The value of information can be measured as a function of both its utility and your risk in maintaining it over time. A holistic understanding of your company's information universe extends to how information can be used at the different points in its life.

Traditionally, records managers determined the lifecycle of information when reviewing bankers boxes of paper records arranged in some structured way based upon a file plan used by employees. So that information from the finance department was aggregated together and retained for about the same time as other finance information. But given how business is transacted today with technologies implemented to make business more efficient, evaluating the lifecycle of this ever-growing mound of data is way more challenging and can't be done in isolation by the records managers. Furthermore, the estimate of value has to be done up front in policy so that those policy rules can be systemically applied when the data is created or received. When developing policy, the following considerations must be assessed to determine the value of information:

- Who has a need to use the information at various points in its lifecycle?
- How long is the information needed to support a business process or activity?
- Does the information have value for planning purposes or future analysis?
- Will information be needed for datamining or analytics purposes?
- Is the information needed in order to fulfill contract obligations?
- Does the information have historical value?
- Does the information have reference value?
- What are the legal requirements for continued retention?
- Is the information considered intellectual property or trade secret?

The value of information, which dictates its lifecycle, needs to be offset by the risks related to its continued retention. For example, the privacy requirements related to information have to be considered when determining the lifecycle. The European Union's General Data Protection Regulation (GDPR) and the 2020 implementation of the 2018 California Consumer Privacy Act, like most privacy regulations, want companies to keep less personal information and for shorter periods of time.

As a leader, you are in a unique position to mobilize the right groups to determine the business value and risks related to the information's lifecycle.

Business Implications

Different parts of the company may have different needs for information, so, garnering a holistic view of value up front from various business units will be essential in getting the value calculus correct and thus manage the lifecycle of information.

As discussed in Rule 11 there is conflict and competition in the uses and needs of information, which should get baked into the assessment of value. For example, data analytics professionals generally want information for longer periods because articulating the future need of the information can be challenging, information security professionals want information for shorter periods so they'll have less to protect.

There is an instinct among employees to over-assess value, which leads to over-retention of information and records; this impulse needs to be resisted. This "packrat-itis" continues to afflict most companies, and that affliction leads to information sprawl and increased risk.

Companies are well served to apply rigor to their information value assessments, otherwise subjective employee-by-employee analysis will lead to inconsistencies and improper retention. Rigor here further contributes to timely disposition of information of limited or no value.

IT should be engaged to understand how the reference value of information in various environments trails off. This can help define the business utility of a piece of information over time, which directly relates to its lifecycle. For example, IT could analyze employee behavior by looking at the last accessed or modified date, in some cases.

Legal Implications

Irrespective of information's normal value and its regular lifecycle, if it is relevant to a lawsuit, audit, or response to a regulator, that information, whether hard copy or electronic, must be preserved. Even if retention requirements would normally allow that information to go away in the ordinary course of business, preservation takes precedence and interrupts the normal destruction of the information.

Changes to the Federal Rules of Civil Procedure made clear that any relevant electronically stored information (ESI is the term used by the legal community since the change to the Federal Rules of Civil Procedure in 2006) must be preserved in the context of a lawsuit. Therefore, while the information value assessment may define business information requirements, in the context of a lawsuit virtually any electronic information could be relevant. So, for example, metadata used to support the audit trail of the information (e.g., create date, modify date, access date) is often not part of the initial information value calculus but may be relevant in a lawsuit.

New privacy and security laws are created regularly which will impact value assessments and legal responsibility. Organizations should stay on top of new laws and regulations. With the passage of new laws, companies need to go back to reassess as the new requirements may impact the value calculus.

Having company policy supported by communication and training is essential to ensure that the organization understands its responsibilities related to the information lifecycle. Executives need to ensure monitoring and enforcement of the policies. For more in-depth discussion on compliance methodology, see Rule 12.

Rule 9

Storage Is Not Cheap

Executive Takeaway

Don't be fooled by assertions that storage is cheap. There is a compelling case for rightsizing your information footprint. Cleaning house takes executive support, money, and effort.

Background

The world is growing the global information footprint at a speed never before seen. Every few hours, the world's volume of data increases by an exabyte, which is the data equivalent of 50,000 years of continuous movies.[1] There are thousands of exabytes of new data created every year and information volumes are growing exponentially.

One often-heard assertion in response to the concern about the growth of information is that storage is cheap. Sound familiar? Let's dispel that myth. Storage is *not* cheap. While the per unit cost of storage may be going down slightly year over year, that reduction in cost is dwarfed by the growth of information. And in real numbers, for

---

1. Randolph A. Kahn, *Why Destruction of Information Is So Difficult and So Essential: The Case for Defensible Disposal*, Business Law Today (Jun. 15, 2018), https://www.americanbar.org/groups/business_law/publications/blt/2018/06/disposal/.

big companies, the overall cost to store their mountain of information amounts to significant dollars. In fact, the information footprint for most companies is doubling every year or two. So, the actual hard cost of the growing information footprint is increasing, which is a compounding recurring cost. What is going down is the cost per unit of storage, but that decline in storage unit cost is a mere few percent per year.

And, it is not just the growth of volume that's relevant when looking at the overall cost of storage. In addition to the hard-quantifiable cost (hardware/software) related to storage, people often minimize the cost related to:

- Privacy and security: There are costs associated with proactively protecting the larger pile and there is risk of more information being exposed if you have a breach.
- Litigation response: The more information, the more time and expense responding to audit, litigation, and investigation, as well as trudging through irrelevant content that could be damaging and/or embarrassing if taken out of context in litigation.
- Employee time: The more unwieldy the pile, the more time-consuming and challenging for employees to find what they need, when they need it to do their job.
- Technical expertise: Paying for technology professionals to babysit outdated information is a bad use of company resources.
- Company exposure and reputation: Exposure of unneeded and outdated information can create signification reputational damage to the company and negatively impact customer loyalty and trust and company valuations. It may also result in substantial regulatory penalties.

Manage the Footprint

As explained in Rule 5, "the more the merrier" approach when it comes to information may be subject to the law of diminishing returns. When employees can't find what they need or the cost of storing information is overwhelming the IT budget, perhaps then it can become inescapably clear that it's time to start better managing the company's information footprint more aggressively.

How to Attack Unneeded Information

How can the case be made that the masses of information need to go away? Defensible disposition is no small task. It is complicated and not without expense (albeit with potentially significant savings). It may require different kinds of diligence depending upon the information at issue. For example, the way you approach the cleanup of disaster recovery tapes that haven't been touched in twenty years will be completely different from determining what messages to purge from an email system that has been used recently and is being migrated.

When information exists that lacks applied retention or disposition rules, it will be essential to understand whether it can be destroyed by communicating with stakeholders: the owner of the information, legal representative who would understand the legal requirements around the information, and any related business unit across the enterprise that might be using that type of information for business or legal purposes.

1. Determine ownership: Determine who is responsible for making decisions on the information at issue. This may be a specific person within a business unit or a business governing council. The owner (steward) is different from the person who runs the system (custodian). IT or third-party providers should not be the decision makers regarding what company information should be retained or destroyed. If there is no business owner for the information, that responsibility will have to be delegated to someone who can make a reasoned business decision on behalf of the company. In today's business environment, this may be more common than you realize.
2. Garner the necessary approvals: To make information go away, you will need buy-in and agreement from the business folks who really own the information. Additionally, you will need approvals from the law department representing the business unit

that owns the information and maybe even other business units that use the information for secondary purposes or regulatory reasons, as in the case of a company's tax department needing to be ready for audit.
3. Determine business value: For the various interested parties within the company, what is the ongoing value of the information? Will the accounting professionals find value in twenty years of information that may have been used by the accounting team decades ago but has been ill-managed for years? Will a database of customer past purchases from years ago be valuable to the big data and analytics team? Are there retention rules or privacy laws that otherwise dictate how this information should be managed or disposed? Are old manufacturing records still valuable decades later? Should retention rules have already initiated disposition? Is the marginal value of the information outweighed by the risk and cost of continued retention? Who understands the information's utility enough to be able to weigh in on these complex questions?
4. Determine legal value: Some lawyers want everything gone tomorrow and others want everything forever. But in the end, neither approach is viable. Lawyers will need to weigh and balance these various issues with business folks to come to a final decision about disposition.
    - Are there any laws or regulations that require the information to be retained for a specific period of time? Has that time been met?
    - Are there any laws or regulation that require disposition because of its content (e.g., privacy)?
    - Are there any contractual obligations that require the information to be retained?
    - Is the information needed to protect legal interests or defend the company? Does the information limit business opportunities?
    - Is there any information that otherwise still needs to be preserved for pending or anticipated audit, litigation, investigations, or other formal matters?

Sufficient diligence should be undertaken to address legal and business value so that lawyers are comfortable with responsibly destroying the information. Lawyers should determine what, if any, documentation is required related to the decision-making process and disposition.
5. Building the right team: Rightsizing your organization should be handled in a coordinated and methodical fashion. Otherwise, there will be inconsistent and potentially bad results. A team should be assembled that represents different interests in order to shepherd the organization through the process.

Rightsizing is essential and cleaning up is much more complex than organizations understand. Build the business case, build the right team, and execute with diligence and rigor.

BUSINESS IMPLICATIONS

Executives need to lead the charge to clean up old and outdated information in order to produce a result that is executed consistently, economically, and expeditiously across the company. In addition, the "keep everything forever" culture must change and the only way that is going to take hold across the enterprise is when it comes from the top. This is essential because users typically want access to all the information; their instinct tells them that everything is important. In that regard, everyone, to a certain degree, has the potential to be a hoarder, and that mindset can't be allowed to obstruct the clean-up process.

Control Information Cost

To control the growth and cost of information, organizations may want to proactively dictate which storage environments are designated as non-record working environments which warrant automated retention and disposition after a short period of time. Records will need to be retained according to laws and regulations and non-record content can be managed based upon business need.

Creators of new information should be tasked with developing and applying information management rules up front so that the lifecycle is predetermined. Such rules should be developed in conjunction with legal, privacy, security, and records management.

Further, where it makes sense, promote the use of managed repositories to the extent practicable and try to get away from new unmanaged pockets of information. When unmanaged pockets are created, apply auditable policies that keep that information on an appropriate lifecycle. The proliferation of repositories that are unmanaged or contain growing piles of obsolete data can more easily pose a privacy or security risk. This requires a substantial change management exercise, especially where employees are wedded to using technologies, that doesn't promote disciplined information management. For example, using traditional email may be easier than using the purpose-built communication tool inside of a system such as SAP.

Clean Up the Crud

Quantify the company's net benefit from disposing of digital information crud. Determining net benefit is complex because certain costs and risks are intangible and can't be precisely quantified. For example, the cost of an information security breach that exposes private information, while potentially huge, is difficult to precisely quantify until it happens. Further, the cost of mitigating risk by having a smaller volume of electronic information is also difficult to precisely quantify. Therefore, it may make sense to be more conservative in your evaluation by considering hard documentable costs and demoting subjective costs and risks.

Rightsizing your information footprint requires diligence, time, expertise, technology, and money to properly and defensibly dispose of large quantities of information. If IT and legal executives are not jointly involved and supporting such efforts the project will likely fail.

Simplified retention rules automatically applied by technology help rightsize the information footprint continually by getting rid of content that no longer has a legal or business value requiring continued retention. Additionally, declaring certain environments as non-record storage locations tells employees where they can store reference materials, draft content, and collaboration files. This promotes automatic and systematic disposition after short periods of time and helps to substantially reduce the footprint of information created that has short-term business and legal value.

When computer systems or applications are to be decommissioned, there must be a process to evaluate what should happen to the information that is resident in those systems. In certain cases, the information can be purged, as it is no longer needed for business or legal purposes. In other cases, the information may be needed for continued retention or litigation response purposes and, if so, the decommissioning process must determine where that information is to be stored according to its particular lifecycle.

Legal Implications

The use of structured applications (SAP, Salesforce) as opposed to unstructured environments (Word, PowerPoint) promotes the creation of consistent and predictable business evidence of transaction, which in turn makes the litigation process less costly and more predictable because the data that is being stored, its location, and what will be generated from it is not a mystery. Contrast that awareness with knowing what is in a Word document before it is found, opened, and reviewed.

Similarly, it is easier to manage, control, and lock down content containing private information when it is stored in a structured environment. Structured environments promote proper disposition of certain classes of information because you know where and what it is. A growing number of privacy laws and regulations require that organizations know where private information is being stored so that it can be better managed throughout its lifecycle. For example, unearthing the presence of social security numbers in a Word document requires the use of complex tools and a process that can be expensive and burdensome, just to find the information type. (For further information related to structured environments, see the data repository cheat sheet below.)

Automating retention promotes compliance and the disposition of information at the end of its lifecycle in a predictable and consistent manner. Further, naming certain storage locations "record" and "non-record" will help automate retention in a methodical and defensible manner.

Data repository cheat sheet

CHARACTERISTICS	RELATIONAL DATABASE	DATA WAREHOUSE	DATA LAKE	DATA MART	OPERATIONAL DATA STORE
Data types	Structured, numerical data, text and dates organized in a relational model	Relational data from transactional systems, operational databases and applications	Structured and unstructured data from sensors, websites, business apps, mobile apps, etc.	Relational data subsets for specific applications	Transactional data from multiple sources
Purpose	Transaction processing	Data stored for business intelligence, batch reporting and data visualization	Big data analytics, machine learning, predictive analytics and data discovery	Data used by a specific user community for analytics	Ingest, integrate, store and prep data for operations or analytics; often feeds a data warehouse
Data capture	Data captured from a single source, such as a transactional system	Data captured from multiple relational sources	Data captured from multiple sources that contain various forms of data	Data typically captured from a data warehouse, but can also be from operational systems and external sources	Data captured from multiple enterprise applications/sources
Data normalization	Uses normalized, static schemas	Denormalized schemas; schema-on-write	Denormalized; schema-on-read	Normalized or denormalized	Denormalized
Benefits	Provides consistent data for critical business applications	Historical data from many sources stored in one place; data is classified with user in mind for accessibility	Data in its native format from diverse sources gives data scientists flexibility in analysis and model development	Easy, fast access to relevant data for specific applications and types of users	Fast queries on smaller amounts of real-time or near-real-time data for reporting and operational decisions
Data quality	Data is organized and consistent	Curated data that is centralized and ready for use in BI and analytics	Raw data that may or may not be curated for use	Highly curated data	Data is cleansed and compliant, but may not be as consistent as in a data warehouse

Rule 10

Know the Expanding Legal and Regulatory Landscape

Executive Takeaway

Executives need to be prepared to navigate an increasingly complex legal minefield when functioning in the new information ecosystem.

Background

The information universe expands along with laws and regulations that seek to regulate information. Laws and regulations in most states and most countries increasingly dictate what your company can and cannot do with information, how long to keep it, how it needs to be secured, how it must be managed, and redress for failing to properly manage it, among other things. Federal regulators like the FTC increasingly manage various complex aspects of privacy and the SEC and FINRA tell financial services companies what technology they can use to run their business and how to properly store electronic information.

Companies should expect that the expanse and complexity of the regulatory ecosystem will continue growing, along with the growing use of electronic information and the proliferation of technology. Companies should expect laws to expand and the best way to manage the expansion is by establishing a structure that allows for coordination and harmonization across jurisdictions and topical areas such as privacy and security that works for them.

The Expanse of Legal Requirements

There is no shortage of laws, regulations, and standards that spell out how to properly manage company information and the consequences of failing to get it right. While the European Union's General Data Protection Regulation (GDPR) has taken center stage in recent years, there are thousands of laws that govern privacy, information security, records retention, destruction of evidence, storage of electronic information, and other aspects of information management.

This expanding landscape of rules isn't going away and running afoul of these laws and regulations is simply not a good thing for your reputation, business, or career. Companies and their management have been penalized, fined, sanctioned, and their executives have personally paid out of pocket, lost careers, and have even been jailed.

In 2019, Google was the first company to be penalized for a GDPR violation: a €50 million ($57 million) fine brought by French regulatory body CNIL. That penalty stings even for a company the size of Google. But what about smaller companies that don't have the resources to comply with this burgeoning body of information law? How will they manage this massive, restrictive, and sometimes conflicting array of rules?

"Assuming, as one would, that both CNIL and Google are well-intentioned, the question nevertheless is, if a company like Google—with all its resources, expertise and economic self-interest in maintaining its businesses legally and responsibly in Europe—can't get it right, what will happen to the many smaller innovative companies . . ."?[1]

---

1. David Doty, *J'Accuse: French Regulatory Body Hits Hard in Its First GDPR Fine*, Forbes (Jan. 28, 2019), https://www.forbes.com/sites/daviddoty/2019/01/28/jaccuse-french-regulatory-body-hits-hard-in-its-first-gdpr-fine/#62de6db37713.

Following the Law of the Land

The decision to do business in a particular jurisdiction is not just about business. When availing your company of a jurisdiction for business, that jurisdiction expects that your company will follow its laws. That means that states expect your company to follow state laws and countries expect your company to follow their laws, as well. Therefore, the broader the expanse of your business footprint the more expansive and complex your legal footprint in which to comply. In an electronic age, the business footprint is usually bigger than most businesses realize. Additionally, there may be industry regulations and best practices that must be followed.

> Recently it was reported that Google was building a filter for internet traffic in China that both violates freedom of expression and U.S. laws but also is contrary to the ethos of Google. But if Google wants to do business in China it needs to act in accordance with their laws even if it assaults the sensibilities of the company.

Make Sense of Conflicting Laws

As the growing tangle of laws and regulations in a widening array of jurisdictions dictate how a company must manage its information, the tracking of potential conflicts and inconsistencies grows complex as well. It can be overwhelming.

For example, just complying with all the laws and regulations on privacy can be anything from a part-time job for one to a cottage industry for many inside your company. The complexity and burden of complying with ever-more country privacy laws was one of the compelling reasons for the EU to pass the GDPR.

For a global company, trying to develop universal policy and compliance practices that comport with the various legal requirements can be a daunting challenge. If the company wanted to review employees' emails for a legitimate purpose, country by country analysis would be needed to grant the company the right to take such action. U.S. employees can waive their right to privacy while a company employee in France does not have that same legal right to waiver. Practically speaking that legal reality limits what compliance professionals may do with employees who are in the same company but are subject to different legal requirements.

Business Implications

Lay It All on the Table

Once you get into the details of information laws and regulations, it becomes clear rather quickly that the various laws may require different policies, actions, and/or technologies in different locations and for different types of information. To proactively address such concerns, sometimes companies will determine all the requirements of all the laws and meld them into a company policy that universally addresses privacy or information security, for example. In other words, rather than apply every law, and every clause of every law, to every type of information, the company creates a matrix that melds all requirements into company policy or guidelines.

It Takes a Team

Increasingly, translating a legal requirement requires that your business, legal, compliance, and IT teams work together. And making that all happen will require visionary leadership that promotes this type of essential collaboration going forward.

Legal Implications

The Letter and the Spirit of the Law

Satisfying the "letter of the law" is not the same as complying with the "spirit of the law" and increasingly businesses need to address both. For example, the SEC Broker Dealer regulation addressing the storage of electronic information seeks to ensure that records will remain available in the unlikely event of a disaster. One part of the regulation states, "[s]tore separately from the original, a duplicate copy of the record stored on any medium acceptable under §240.17a-4 for the time required." When disaster struck, it became painfully clear that certain financial firms did not follow the "spirit of the law" by storing a copy of required records on a separate floor of the same building, satisfying only the "letter of the law." Industry best practice for disaster recovery requires that the two record copies be stored miles apart and on different systems in the unlikely event of disaster.

The Evolution of the Custodian

Historically, records management dealt with records, and extraneous papers went away in the ordinary course of business as trash. With reliance upon electronic records or computer-generated records, increasingly the IT department became the unexpected custodian creating new complexities and issues. We are now entering a new phase where an unsuspecting business unit or third party may be in possession of company information. For example, consider that every IoT implementation likely grants some third-party access to or use of what the company may consider its own information. Review Rule 17 on IoT for further discussion.

> The EU went live with the GDPR directives (General Data Protection Regulation) in 2018, which among other things dictates that those with access to or are storing EU residents' data have an obligation to keep the information only as long as its original use required.[2]

---

2. William Long and Vishnu Shankar, *The Impact of the GDPR on the Retention of Personal Data*, September 2016 Cyber Security Law & Practice, https://www.sidley.com/-/media/publications/cslp-september-2016-1516.pdf.

Rule 11

Bridge Worlds and Navigate Conflicts

Executive Takeaway

Areas within the organization have different interests that drive different needs and uses for the same information. Those needs and interests may dictate a different approach to managing the information. Company leadership needs to understand the conflicts and competition in its midst and help navigate it.

Background

Over the past few decades, much of the information a business created went from existing exclusively on paper to exclusively in electronic form. Information is now easier to send, gather, share, collaborate on, and analyze, promoting business efficiency. It is also easier to transmit mistakenly, access improperly, and hack. Further, electronic information proliferates in unintended ways and may be seen by unintended recipients. It can also stick around way past its expiration date without deteriorating and can propagate uncontrollably, posing new global privacy and information security risks.

While the global electronic information footprint has grown exponentially, the laws and regulations that sought to regulate the new electronic universe also evolved. There are more and more laws telling companies what to do with their information from the perspective of privacy, information security, storage, destruction, retention, and discovery. Privacy professionals want to keep less information for shorter periods of time in part because the law requires it and in part because risk goes up the more information is kept and the longer it is kept. And that risk comes in various forms, from information security, to theft of IP, to privacy breach.

Meanwhile, in that same company where privacy professionals push to keep less, business folks working on data-intensive projects that can redefine the direction of the business are pushing to keep more information for longer and longer. What if the information is a treasure trove, describing customer behavior or product preferences? What if the information could be used for resource planning—a change of course from its original intended use. Will the law conflict with the company building the next big thing? What if we destroy information containing golden nuggets of value?

These conflicts now pop up routinely and resolving them poorly can mean stifling innovation or exposing the company to unneeded risk. Leadership is needed to set the right tone and settle disputes appropriately.

Business units should talk about information needs, and when conflicts arise try to negotiate a resolution to the conflict that accommodates everyone's needs. So, if data is needed for data mining purposes but retention would run afoul of an EU privacy rule, then perhaps the information can be anonymized to preempt the privacy concerns, for example. All business units, including operations, legal, IT, compliance, and regulatory affairs should have a voice at the table to clearly define risks and benefits related to the information at issue.

What follows is an example of how different business units, roles, and people in the company use information differently, which changes their view on how to manage the same information. It is important to keep in mind that depending upon where you sit in the company, your need for information may be diametrically opposed to someone across the company in a different function or business unit.

The examples capture the representative mindset of different people in the organization:

Conflict 1:
Litigator: Ensure information is available for potential litigation. IT data steward: Continuing to maintain a decommissioned system is expensive and unnecessary.

Conflict 2:
Data Scientist: A bigger data sample from a longer time-range yields more useful analytics. Privacy Professional: Keep personal information only as long as needed for its original intended business purpose.

Conflict 3:
Marketer: We absolutely need to keep marketing materials to understand our brand histories. Other Marketer: Why is the storage of all of that information in our budget?

Conflict 4:
Contracts Lawyer: We need to keep all information and documents (including drafts) related to a particular transaction into the future without an end point. Records Retention Professional: The retention of only the final records is to be retained for only as long as the Records Retention Schedule dictates.

There may be lawyers in your midst along with marketers, privacy professionals, records managers, accountants, and even data scientists who see the opportunities and risks in your information landscape very differently. "Doing right by the company" can be interpreted in very different ways—think of how litigation collection and information systems strategies might diverge. For example, lawyers want everything retained and information systems professionals want antiquated systems to go away. They need to take each other's requirements into account. It is up to you as leader to set a tone that helps these and other competing forces to find your company's sweet spot between opportunity and risk when these conflicts arise. And they will, increasingly, as laws governing information grow in scope and instances of information mismanagement failures increase as well.

For example, the GDPR seeks to have as little information related to individuals kept for only as long as its original intended purpose. That regulation puts retention professionals on notice that existing retention schedules may be insufficient, and they may need to ensure retention periods are as short as possible. Contemporaneously, U.S. marketers are seeking to broaden their analytics business processes looking at European buying habits to maximize sales and profitability. Clearly, the same information may be implicated in both situations and someone needs to navigate its potential conflict to maximize business and mitigate risk.

An executive will need to address the questions below to resolve the conflict:

1. Which business unit or function has an interest in the conflict?
2. What executive(s) has authority and responsibility to navigate the conflicts? This will vary company to company, business unit to business unit, and even executive to executive.
3. Who owns the business problem?
4. Which attorney in the law department has authority to speak on the issue?
5. Are there any applicable laws or regulations?
6. Is there a way to compromise or resolve the apparent conflict without impacting business value or increasing risk (e.g., anonymize individuals' data to remove privacy concerns)?
7. Which business units and/or individuals will need to agree to the action?
8. Which lawyers need to determine what documentation of the process should be retained?
9. Which lawyer should approve of the action?

10. Is there any action that can be taken to mitigate against the risk of harm from the decision (e.g., insurance)?

There may not be one-size-fits-all answers to these kinds of issues. What is clear is that information is valuable and there are lots of ways to exploit its value. However, every time a new use of that same information is considered the above issues need to be addressed.

BUSINESS IMPLICATIONS

One of the axioms of information is to always limit access to only those who have an absolute need and right to see, use, and access the information. Following this axiom will help minimize conflicts.

Evaluate Information before Using It in a New Way

Before using information in any way other than its original intended purpose, companies must evaluate whether or not the risk and liability of its new use outweighs its potential benefit to the company. In other words, just because you can use it, doesn't mean you should. Facebook is a great cautionary tale as a big part of their business model depends on selling and sharing information. There is no question that there may be some value in selling it, but what is the downside if you breach the trust of your customers. In today's age it is not enough to seek to harness the value of information; it has to be weighed against the downside risk. Managing the potential conflict of using information for secondary purposes requires weighing and balancing myriad competing interests.

Your transactional information may have value after it is created for new uses like predictive modeling in your marketing department, product planning purposes by your suppliers, or for marketing and selling of related products or services by another company. For example, if you sell automobiles, a company that offers repair services would probably have an interest in buying your sales information. There is value in selling the information but what are the risks? Could that company take the sales information and sell it to one of your automotive competitors? If a third-party purchaser of the data follows up with your customers, will your customers deem it a breach of trust or annoying encroachment that will otherwise impact the trust you've built or your reputation? Before considering the information for new uses, organizations must weigh the value and risk.

- Is the information trade secret or covered by intellectual property rights?
- What is the new use for the information?
- Who is going to use it—another business unit and third party?
- Is it leaving the company?
- Can using the information in a new way damage the company (i.e., reputation, competition, financially)?
- Are there laws or regulations that tell you that you can't?
- Are there contract terms that will be violated if you share it or repurpose it?

There may not always be hard and fast answers to the questions above, but executives are going to have to navigate the benefits and risks of using and reusing and possibly selling the information.

Conflicts Go beyond Official Company Records

Analysis of big data often involves non-record information. That information might be stored in various kinds of unstructured collaboration and communication environments which may not be subject to records retention rules and regulations mandating specific disposition at a particular point in time. Even though this data may contain significant value when analyzed, it is typically hard to classify and generally defies easy organization. For this class of information, if anyone owns the information it is likely the employee, at best. It isn't practical to work with thousands of employees to resolve conflicts, so organizations need to delegate ownership to the appropriate executives that will be charged with making decisions on behalf of the masses.

Non-records may be subject to privacy laws, but the company may not even know where the data exists. Let's say that three months ago, personally identifiable information was extracted from the HR system and stored in a big data repository for trending purposes not related to the HR function. How will this information be erased if and when an individual requests that he be forgotten, in accordance with Europe's GDPR, if that law applies? Who knows that it is in the big data repository? If the information is around, even if the records to which it relates have been destroyed in the ordinary course of business pursuant to company policy, then the information may still be discoverable in the context of a lawsuit. So just because it was used for predictive analytics purposes, it can still have a privacy or information security impact if things go bad.

Conflicts may involve compliance personnel wanting information kept in conformity with the company's records retention schedule while IT storage executives want to clean house immediately to reduce storage that incurs costs that rise dramatically with volumes. Litigation lawyers may want all information preserved while the CIO complains that server performance will be cut in half.

Balancing risks and benefits related to the management of information is a real challenge for most organizations today and requires an information governance strategy to address it.

Legal Implications

Know Your Risk Appetite

Organizations cannot manage information conflicts without their being known and evaluated in a methodical way with input from the law department and compliance professionals. If there is no structure to resolve conflicts, different business units may take different or inconsistent action that has not been sufficiently vetted and may impact the company.

Conflicts between Business Needs and Law

To make better decisions and to stay competitive, businesses need to analyze large and complex data sets known as big data. Big data analytics require collecting and storing data over time to identify patterns, correlations, and trends and to analyze the trends to inform business decisions. For example, businesses that have consumer interaction rely on big data to optimize customer service, improve products or services, and forecast future demand. What if laws and regulations don't allow a business to retain the data that is needed to forecast the future? Laws may limit how companies can use this type of data in the future. Finding a balance or a solution that complies with laws and regulations without impacting the business value that can be harnessed from big data is an enterprise challenge that needs to be addressed by various players in the organization—legal, IT, compliance, security, and privacy among them.

The Right to Be Forgotten

GDPR generally gives individuals the right to request that their personal data be erased where it is no longer needed for its original purpose.[1] This means that, upon request, the company may be forced to erase personal data related to the individual, wherever it is stored, unless an exception exists. Yet, certain U.S. laws dictate different results. For example, many companies must retain industry-related records for a certain period of time, as in the Fair Labor Standards Act,[2] which requires employers to retain payroll records for at least three years, and the Equal Employment Opportunity Commission[3] requires private employers to retain personnel records for one year after the end of employment. Therefore, a company trying to make sense of these seemingly inconsistent legal requirements by having

---

1. *See* GDPR, Art. 17(1); Art. 12(3).
2. *See* Fair Labor Standards Act (29 C.F.R. §516.5(a)).
3. *See* Equal Employment Opportunity Commission (29 C.F.R. §1602(A)(1)).

one global policy will face a challenge that requires legal guidance to delicately navigate the conflict.

Making GDPR compliance work with U.S. law will require navigating or negotiating seemingly inconsistent legal requirements. More specifically, when it comes to personal information you must ensure that you're storing it for a legitimate business reason and retaining as little as possible for as short a term as possible to satisfy the spirit of privacy requirements and information security needs.

Retention Requirements

In order to make the rules for retaining and destroying information easier to implement, companies may be using a "big bucket" approach to retention. A big bucket retention rule aggregates several retention rules into one rule for ease of use. This will require mapping many regulations to one retention rule to determine the new retention period. For example, if most related regulations call for retention at ten years and the rest call for a six-year retention, someone, including someone the law department, will need to navigate this conflict. This big bucket approach will more likely enhance compliance by making fewer rules and making them easier to learn and apply.

Rule 12

Build and Support a Compliance Culture

Executive Takeaway

Mistakes will happen. Transgressions will happen. Failure will happen. Implement compliance methodology to protect the company from information failures. Compliance methodology helps institutionalize "reasonableness."

Background

Though it may seem like ancient history, in 2002 the venerable Arthur Andersen evaporated in large part due to management failing to lead when a couple of employees sought to destroy evidence to cover their tracks in the Enron debacle. Actually, a lawyer and a partner reminded employees to follow the retention schedule after they learned of allegations of an accounting failure—a directive that all but ensured that records were destroyed. As that act became known to the court of public opinion its clients lost trust in the company and this precipitated the firm's rapid decline. Had management done the right thing, which was to ensure that all potentially relevant evidence was preserved at the first sign of trouble, Andersen would likely still be in business. That doesn't mean that there wouldn't have been consequences in their accounting failure in the Enron case, but it may not have meant the end to one of the largest accounting firms in the world. If select employees seek to take action in violation of

> Uber is in hot water after a cover-up scandal involving a major security breach.
>
> The ride-hailing company paid hackers $100,000 to cover up a cyberattack that exposed 57 million people's personal data in October 2016, *Bloomberg* reported Tuesday. And, while passengers and drivers only found out this week, ex-CEO Travis Kalanick reportedly found out about the breach last year.[1]

company policy and good management, a compliance process may insulate the company from the bad act.

Think of some of the most recent cases of misconduct at Wells Fargo, Volkswagen, and Uber. In each case there is a component of the failure that involves information that substantially impacts a legal claim, regulatory matter, and how the public sees these companies. While companies can't inoculate against bad acts of employees, compliance methodology (described below) helps insulate the company or mitigate the penalty.

There are all sorts of ways companies simply make mistakes or fail to properly protect their information assets. When companies and their executives are judged, a court invariably evaluates what the company and its leaders did right and what they did wrong and whether the actions were timely and reasonable.

A compliance culture has a few main components. Employees need to understand the company's expectations of them, embodied in its policies and processes. They need to know that the organization will support them when they do the right thing. They need to know that there will be consequences if the employee does not do the right thing. And they need to know that there are avenues for speaking up about misconduct and that the company is not just talking the talk.

---

1. Kate Taylor and Benjamin Goggin, *49 of the Biggest Scandals in Uber's History*, Business Insider (May 10, 2019), https://www.businessinsider.com/uber-company-scandals-and-controversies-2017-11.

Given the volume of information and the complexity of laws and challenges that employees face, it is essential that organizations implement compliance methodology as a means to mitigate the downside of failures as a way for organizations to help employees operationalize doing the right thing.

What Is Compliance Methodology?

Modern corporate compliance programs evolved out of the U.S. Federal Sentencing Guidelines: Sentencing of Organizations (Chapter 8),[2] which laid out criteria for evaluating a corporation if and when it is prosecuted for some criminal wrong like destruction of evidence. For companies that don't use compliance methodology this section helps lay out the major components, but even if your company does, it is often not applied to information-related activities. Or, information-related activities are not perceived as priority. And, given the growing risk from information disasters, applying the methodology to all information activities is more important than ever. If you act reasonably and take reasonable precautions, the courts are less likely to penalize your company as they understand that no company can be perfect day in and day out. That is especially true in managing information where failure can be common—be it privacy, information security, litigation response, or records retention. In early 2019, The Department of Justice Criminal Division updated a guidance document for white-collar prosecutors on the evaluation of corporate compliance programs, entitled "The Evaluation of Corporate Compliance Programs."[3] The document "seeks to better harmonize the guidance with other Department guidance and standards while providing additional context to the multifactor analysis of a company's compliance program."

---

2. *See* https://www.ussc.gov/guidelines/2018-guidelines-manual/2018-chapter-8.

3. *See* Department of Justice Evaluation of Corporate Compliance Programs, March 2019. https://www.justice.gov/criminal-fraud/page/file/937501/download.

Components of Compliance Methodology

The Seven Hard Criteria of Compliance Methodology:

1. Policies and directives telling employees what to do and what not to do
2. Proper and timely executive action
3. Delegation throughout the organization of policy, responsibilities, conduct, etc.
4. Communication and Training
5. Auditing and Monitoring
6. Consistent Enforcement
7. Continuous Improvement[4]

BUSINESS IMPLICATIONS

Compliance Methodology bakes "reasonableness" into business processes that can help employees get it right and protect the company when they don't. The law department should be consulted when addressing how the actions might be perceived and determining how the company understands "what is reasonable."

Building a compliance culture within the business units of your company helps address common information failures more readily. For issues like information security and privacy that confound employees and impact companies regularly, a compliance culture would help reduce failure by routinizing compliance through regular training, communication, and auditing, to help mitigate the risk.

To minimize impact to employees, build Compliance into all information processes. That helps make it transparent and seamless to the employees. Allow technology to do the heavy lifting by applying the rules that will unburden employees and promote compliance—technology is often better than people at managing information. And

---

4. *See* Randolph Kahn and Barclay T. Blair, *Information Nation: Seven Keys to Information Compliance* (2009).

RULE 12: BUILD AND SUPPORT A COMPLIANCE CULTURE

> Facebook Inc. has been under scrutiny for months over its handling of personal data, but it has been haggling with financial firms over its access to sensitive financial data for years.[5]

further, using technology to do what employees used to do may be considered by courts and regulators as reasonable, if not essential. In the context of litigation, if companies don't use technology to unearth potentially relevant information, a court might consider it neglectful given the utility and low cost.

Perhaps most importantly, building information compliance into your company creates a guide for employees and the company to get it right. What that may mean is that customer's information is protected more thoroughly and more often; information security failures are less frequent or painful; company intellectual property and trade secrets information are better protected; and customer support is enhanced by the company's representatives readily finding customer information.

Legal Implications

Compliance methodology may be your company's get out of jail free card when failure happens as it can demonstrate that your company sought to be a good corporate citizen and do the right thing even if failure happened.

Demonstration to a court or a regulator that a pattern of good behavior exists in the face of some information failure tends to minimize penalties.

---

5. Anna Maria Andriotis and Emily Glazer, *Facebook Sought Access to Financial Firms' Customer Data for Years*, Wall Street Journal (Sep. 18, 2018), https://www.marketwatch.com/story/facebook-sought-access-to-financial-firms-customer-data-for-years-2018-09-18?rss=1%3Fsiteid%3Drss&rss=1.

Rule 13

Empower Your Organization to Unlock Answers

Executive Takeaway

Understand the value of tools and expertise that can retrieve answers from masses of information. The insights, connections, and predictions derived by these tools can revolutionize how you see your business.

Background

There are information analyzing tools that are purpose-built to analyze large volumes of data in databases or in unstructured content like Microsoft Office documents or social media. That analysis can be used to improve your business, reduce cost, and increase customer satisfaction. This Rule will primarily focus on these types of technologies. However, there are technologies that are being used today that are very complex and integrated into products such as vehicle brake systems, self-driving cars, implantable medical devices, and robots that learn to "think" like humans and act as independently as humans. These more complex technologies will only be covered at a high-level in this Rule.

The Tools Are Getting More Powerful

It has always been a challenge to analyze volumes of information from different sources. Traditional, relational database technology, around since the 1980s, is meant to handle well-structured transactional data.

DATA SCIENTISTS CAN UNLOCK ANSWERS

Data Science

A data scientist works with sets of data from inside or outside the company. The person in this role organizes or "cleans" the data for quality, preparing it for analysis, and then extracts business meaning from it using a toolbox that includes data mining and business intelligence. High quality data is checked for validity, accuracy, completeness, consistency, and uniformity.

Data Mining

Data mining is the process of finding patterns, correlations, and trends using statistical analysis.

Business Intelligence

Business intelligence is answering a business question by taking data and making it more easily digestible. Business intelligence includes the applications, infrastructure, and best practices that are required to analyze information, specifically to make business decisions and improve business performance.

COMPUTING CAN DO THE HEAVY LIFTING

Artificial Intelligence (AI)

AI involves cognitive functioning or "reasoning" done by the computer as opposed to a person. It is usually an algorithm or set of instructions that does that "heavy lifting." AI can learn, come to conclusions, and analyze data.

Machine Learning

Machine learning is an area of AI where systems automatically learn and continue to improve performance over time without additional programming.

GET A BIGGER HAYSTACK, FIND MORE NEEDLES

Big Data

Large quantities of data are constantly being churned out by transactional systems, social media, and other sources both inside and outside the organization. Big data is about analyzing those information volumes using the power of computing.

A PICTURE IS WORTH A BILLION BYTES

Data Visualization

Insights must be communicated to be used, data visualization is a way to communicate data or findings through graphs and other visual depictions.

Companies now benefit from more powerful tools and methods used to analyze large sets of data from various sources to find patterns, correlations, and trends and deliver real competitive advantage. These tasks would be overwhelming for humans to tackle on their own. Your company can and likely is already leveraging aspects of the revolution in artificial intelligence, such as machine learning and algorithms, to dive deeper and find answers that even an army of humans alone cannot.

Let Algorithms Do the Heavy Lifting

We are undergoing a great technical leap where algorithms—essentially a set of steps a computer needs to solve a problem—answer more and more complex problems of business and day-to-day life. This type of artificial intelligence has an advantage over humans because it can analyze small, subtle patterns of information and add millions or trillions of the patterns together to get a macro analysis of all the patterns.

Let the Machines Learn and Improve at Getting Your Answers

It used to be said that you can't get a computer to do what it isn't programmed to do. That's no longer the case. Algorithms can now edit a computer's approach based on information it has analyzed, not just the information used to program it directly. Machine learning is a way for programs to learn and improve from information that is run through them automatically. The knowledge hidden in big data can provide the foundation and the initial training that is necessary for these types of technological solutions to come to conclusions.

> A health insurance company wants to build a system that promotes better long-term health of its insureds, and of course save money along the way. If it could figure out what or who is bringing about better health outcomes through care and treatment provided, it could develop a new business model that rewards providers for those better outcomes. But how to crunch through the hundreds of diagnoses, in hundreds of locations, with thousands of providers, conducted on hundreds of thousands of patients over decades, in addition to many other variables that may be in play? There is no human way to reasonably evaluate all that information and extract the answers needed: who is delivering better medical care and providing better outcomes. But technology now can and does routinely help with these types of business problems.
>
> Applying analysis technology to all the outcomes of all the diagnoses across the various providers and geographic locations, the technology can help determine the quicker, better patient outcomes for gall bladder surgery, or hip replacement, or skin cancer treatment, or any treated malady. By analyzing the data, the insurance company can reward the providers with positive outcomes and stop utilizing underperformers. It can also publish findings to help practitioners improve. But that is just one example of endless issues now being solved with code.

Where Does the Information Come From?

Big data is one of those concepts that helps illustrate the simplicity, complexity, and power of today's technology landscape. Data is now created everywhere, from transactions on big hardware to interactions on our phones, and these large data sets can reveal patterns and provide insight. Combining data from diverse sources can make that insight downright predictive in some cases—down to knowing a customer's next move (predictive analytics). Not leveraging the tools that provide your competitors with insight can leave you at a disadvantage. But there are a few constraining factors. For example, the use of this valuable data and resulting insight can be seen as intrusive on a personal level. In some cases, it can even conflict with the principles underlying privacy laws, such as the EU's GDPR, if not handled correctly.

Business Implications

Select the Right Tool

Different kinds of tools or solutions can be leveraged depending on the kind of problem to be solved. Knowing what the data set is and what you are seeking to solve makes selecting the tools much easier. If you have a discovery problem to solve, there are purpose-built tools designed to solve it. If you are trying to classify data, there are several kinds of tools that can do the job. However, no off-the-shelf solution is a panacea for all information analysis problems.

The selection of an analysis tool starts with the business problem definition or a challenge that has to be addressed. Clearly defining the need is essential to getting to the right answer and applying the right tool that will assist in finding it. The lack of problem definition can equate to a pile of data whose real value is specious.

Resist Shiny Objects

Technology folks are often accused of buying technology because it's cool; in the information analysis space there are cool new technologies and tools being developed all the time. Resist buying the next new tool unless there is a real business challenge that it can solve. Commit to finding the right tool or service provider that addresses your current business challenge and that will be able to support your long-term business and IT strategy. Use your knowledge of business needs across the enterprise to guide your organization in buying the fewest tools necessary to support your needs.

Acquire the Expertise

There is no one resource that can run all information-analysis-related initiatives in a company. The staff ranges from the very technical resources that understand the technology details to the artificial intelligence process resources that actually apply and tweak the technology to address a specific business problem. Companies are bolstering their resources to meet the demand of analyzing and understanding company data through the use of technology.

LEGAL IMPLICATIONS

The future value of information creates new risks and issues that need to be addressed. For most businesses, the future value requires that information be retained—sometimes for long periods of time. Increasingly, with information security and privacy risks on the rise, laws and good business practices require companies keep less information for shorter periods of time. That flies in the face of the needs of the big data business professionals who want more information for longer periods of time as they don't know what information will be valuable.

Privacy and Trust

One significant issue with analysis or artificial intelligence tools is that for these tools to work, they need big piles of information to crawl through and analyze. However, the more information in the piles the greater the privacy or information security risk. So, organizations should be mindful about what is retained, how it is protected, and how it is used. Increasingly, having clear policies on information use, management, and retention, and following them is essential to mitigating risk. Securely getting rid of outdated or unneeded information also helps mitigate the privacy and information security risk.

If It's Around, It's Likely Discoverable

Any information that is potentially relevant to a legal matter is subject to discovery. Your company may have to produce that information in the context of a lawsuit. So even if information was supposed to be destroyed for records retention purposes, if it still exists, even for analytical reasons, it may be discoverable.

Watch Out for Bias in Algorithms

One of unintended consequences of algorithm use is that it can unintentionally discriminate against protected populations. Say an insurance company is using an analysis tool to assist in underwriting and the tool decided that certain profiles should not be covered due to high incidence of cancer in the area. What if the population is comprised of one ethnic group and in a low-income area? Even though no one directed the computer, it nonetheless concluded that few inhabitants in certain zip codes should be covered. That is not to say the tool seeks to discriminate but rather there is a disparate impact on the protected population from something the algorithm

> [AI] models are no more objective than the people who devise and build them. The model must be trained using relevant and correct data and it must learn which data to emphasize. The model must not emphasize information relating to racial or ethnic origin, political opinion, religion or belief, trade union membership, genetic status, health status, or sexual orientation if this would lead to arbitrary discriminatory treatment. If it is suspected, or claimed, that use of a model will entail unfair or discriminatory results, the Data Protection Authority [in a given country] can investigate whether the principle of fairness has been safeguarded in the processing of personal data.[1]

---

1. *Artificial Intelligence and Privacy*, The Norwegian Data Protection Authority (2018), https://iapp.org/media/pdf/resource_center/ai-and-privacy.pdf.

does. This concern is real for some as claims arise of the screening and limiting of conservative political views on Twitter or Facebook, for example, or that Google's search engines discriminate.

> AI systems trained exclusively on the past are doomed to repeat it.
> —Ken Goldberg, UC Berkeley[2]

Encrypt and Anonymize to Protect Privacy

One way to protect privacy is to anonymize the information. That means taking out or hiding the personal identifiable information so that if it gets hacked or exposed, personal information is not viewable and the company is not responsible for failing to properly protect the information. As of March 2018, all fifty states have data breach laws; in this environment taking extra precautions to protect information assets is legally prudent in addition to being the right thing to do.

Obscuring information with encryption technologies while company information is in transit or at rest has become increasingly important. Making information incapable of being viewed once encrypted is essential in today's world where hacking and theft of information has become big business. For information stored in your databases or the cloud, risk of loss goes down substantially when information is encrypted. The issue for the big data folks is that encrypted databases are harder to work with. Refer to Rule 11 for more on different perspectives on information use across your organization.

---

2. "How AI and Humans Can Work Together," MIT Sloan Management Review Webinar, Thursday, February 28, 2019, Ken Goldberg.

Rule 14

Treat Privacy Like Your Company's Reputation Depends on It

Executive Takeaway

Put information privacy in the right perspective. Protecting privacy is about protecting people *and* protecting your company's reputation.

Background

The Privacy Regulatory Landscape Is Full

It seems that a new privacy-related law is passed every day somewhere in the world telling businesses how to manage personal and private information and what will happen if they fail. Some of the most recent are Europe's General Data Privacy Regulation (GDPR), Brazil's General Data Protection Law (LGPD), and the State of California's Consumer Privacy Act. The privacy laws vary slightly but at minimum they generally require that your company knows what private and personal information is collected, how it is protected and managed, and when and how it must be destroyed.

Is Privacy a Human Right?

Countries have taken various approaches to protecting privacy, but much of the landscape seems to be converging. The EU, which treats privacy as a human right, created the GDPR; in effect since May

> **GDPR's Seven Principles:**
> 1. Lawfulness, fairness, and transparency
> 2. Purpose limitation
> 3. Data minimization
> 4. Accuracy
> 5. Storage limitation
> 6. Integrity and confidentiality (security)
> 7. Accountability

2018, it is a sweeping set of rules that governs the way personal information is collected, stored, and used. At its core the GDPR means to give people control over information about them. In a GDPR world, information that identifies you as an individual is not collected without your consent, can be deleted or updated at your request, and must respect your right to be forgotten.

The United States Has Seen Privacy as a Consumer Issue

While the Federal Trade Commission regulates privacy, primarily to protect the consumer, generally speaking, the United States seeks to address privacy sectorally: through regulators focused on specific industries. For example, privacy rules for healthcare, banking, and telemarketing are regulated by a variety of agencies and laws (HIPAA, Gramm-Leach-Bliley Act, Telemarketing Sales Rule, and others). U.S. law generally provides a variety of protections related to personal or private information but does not rise to the level of human right protection in the United States as it does in Europe. Therefore, in the business context, employers regularly ask their employees to agree to waive their right to privacy when using company technology and telecommunications systems.

But Things Are Changing

As of this writing, Congress is looking to create a federal privacy law, limiting data collection by organizations and making collection more transparent, which feels a bit more like the way the European laws regulate privacy. Similarly, the new California Consumer Privacy Act of 2018, which becomes law in 2020, also feels more like GDPR than past U.S. laws.

Consequences for Failure Are Getting Bigger

There have been countless stories in recent years where a company runs afoul of a law or regulations or industry rule related to privacy and faces the wrath of a court or regulator or even the court of public opinion. Companies should expect to face larger and more impactful penalties for privacy information infractions going forward. In this environment failure to protect personal information will be met not only with impact to the bottom line but with further impact to reputation. Penalties can be in the hundreds of millions of dollars. According to the GDPR administrative fines can be, "[u]p to €20 million, or 4% of a company's worldwide annual revenue of the prior financial year, whichever is higher."[1]

> Google for months kept secret a bug that imperiled the personal data of Google+ users.[2]

Everyone Is a Manager of Personal Information

Protecting privacy is a team sport requiring ongoing vigilance from the entire enterprise and all employees. To truly to get on top of privacy requires your company creating a privacy-sensitive culture. That may entail tasking an executive with overall privacy management responsibility for your company as well as rolling out a privacy

---

1. *See* GDPR at https://www.gdpreu.org/compliance/fines-and-penalties/.

2. Craig Timberg, Renae Merle, and Cat Zakrzewski, *Google for Months Kept Secret a Bug That Imperiled the Personal Data of Google+ Users*, The Washington Post (Oct. 8, 2018), https://www.washingtonpost.com/technology/2018/10/08/google-overhauls-privacy-rules-after-discovering-exposure-user-data/?noredirect=on&utm_term=.1508e5f7a74b.

program, including policies and training communicating the importance of privacy and auditing to ensure that employees understand and follow company policies.

Business Implications

There are many business implications to having access to and working with private information. What follows is a partial list of essential privacy considerations that business executives need to proactively navigate with their law departments.

- Privacy management should be built into your business processes by design.
- Privacy should be baked into systems and automated to the extent possible; leave employees out to the extent that you can.
- Collect information on individuals fairly and with their consent. If you specified a use for the data when you collected it, limit use to that purpose.
- Make sure customers and employees understand how their personal information is going to be used, that they sign off on that use, and that you retain proof of their consent.
- Privacy policies tend to be dense and complex, so translate policy into understandable directives that the average employee can follow.
- Some executive needs to be tasked with ensuring that all business units are applying policy consistently.
- Proactively assess all new data sources that contain private information to ensure that the management of the information complies with laws and regulations.
- Your organization should know what private information is collected, where it is stored, how it is protected, and how and when it is disposed of.
- The company should have a routinized response to mitigate risk related to personal information that is being improperly managed in a technology or system.

- An executive needs to make sure that all third-party contracts that give access to any private information are managed appropriately.
- If the company has the ability to share or sell the private information, is that ability memorialized in contract?
- Are third parties with access to your private information complying with agreed-upon terms for use of that information?
- Ensure that there is a process to identify potential breaches and determine if there is an obligation to notify the public or those potentially impacted about the breach.
- Companies should limit the number of locations where they store company information, especially those containing private information as it is easier to protect the information in fewer places.
- Executives and lawyers should manage conflicting legal requirements in a global company context and, specifically, the transferring of data across jurisdictions.
- Business folks should keep as little private information for as short a period of time as they can and, in any event, no longer than the company's retention rules.
- Private information should be properly disposed of when it is no longer immediately needed.

Keep It Simple

Companies' privacy policies and privacy notices often fail because they are too long, too complex and require a lawyer to understand them. All information-related policies, notices, and related directives should seek to be short, simple, and understood by the average person.

A *privacy policy* is an internally focused statement, directing employees in protecting information in line with the company's principles.

A *privacy notice* is an external statement (seen on corporate websites, for example) that explains to customers, site visitors, regulators, and other stakeholders what the company does with personal information.

Because companies use customer or employee information in business regularly, they sometimes become desensitized to the importance of managing the privacy implications. Therefore, it is essential that business executives bake privacy management into their business processes as their bottom line and reputation depend upon it.

LEGAL IMPLICATIONS

The legal and business implication of managing privacy are inextricably linked. See "Business Implications" above to address legal and compliance issues.

Rule 15

Information Security: Protect the Crown Jewels

Executive Takeaway

Make information security a priority. The value of information security goes beyond protecting your business from interruption. Successful attacks can destroy trust.

Background

The world of information security has become rather sophisticated. Information security is implemented and maintained to protect the information crown jewels and the company IP that dwells within your company's environment. Those assets have become a persistent and potentially valuable target for thieves, criminal gangs, governments, and others hell-bent on either stealing, disrupting, or embarrassing. What follows is a brief overview of some of the kinds of attacks that your company is likely facing. Understand that new kinds of attacks morph daily, making the risk so much more challenging.

The Never-Ending Assault

Cyberattacks and malware seek to get into your network, grab data, disrupt, spy, or lie-in-wait to do something nefarious in the future. While attacks on company's security have increased in sophistication over time, many cyberattacks are successful because they bombard organizations with thousands or even millions of malicious assaults just to find a way into company computers. There are endless examples in the news in which companies have been substantially impacted by one simple hack. Given the big business nature of cyberattacks today, companies should expect the sophistication of the cybercriminal to evolve and the onslaught to continue.

The Internet of Things (IoT)

The IoT is the proliferation of devices embedded with software and sensors. That includes devices like Fitbit, implantable medical devices, smart connected vehicles, appliances, sports monitors, connected electronic devices, smart homes, connected health, robots, infrastructure sensors, music devices, and others. These devices are connected to the internet and they collect and transmit information. IoT devices are increasingly interconnected and accessible, but often have limited security, making information even more vulnerable to cyberattacks and making it harder for your organization to calculate risk. We're on track for an explosion of IoT devices, and that translates into greater risk as more and more organizations use IoT devices to augment traditional business processes.

Starting in 2020, California's IoT CyberSecurity Law, passed in 2018, requires smart device manufacturers to equip devices with reasonable security features to protect against hacking and inappropriate disclosure of information.

Economic Espionage as a Service

You can buy almost anything on the dark web that you cannot buy on the mainstream web, such as stolen credit card numbers, stolen IP, and even IP thieves themselves. "Economic espionage attacks can be aided by espionage-as-a-service offerings that are readily available in cybercriminal underground forums and markets and the Deep Web. Attackers can easily buy the tools they need to spy on and exfiltrate highly confidential corporate data or 'company crown

RULE 15: INFORMATION SECURITY: PROTECT THE CROWN JEWELS

> Economic espionage (sometimes called industrial espionage) is the theft of companies' intellectual property, know-how, and trade secrets. After terrorism, it's the greatest national security concern of the FBI. According to General Keith Alexander, formerly the US's top cyber-warrior, "[t]he loss of industrial information and intellectual property through cyber espionage constitutes the 'greatest transfer of wealth in history.'"[1]

jewels' from rivals. They can even hire hackers to do the actual spying for them," according to Trend Micro.[2]

The Problem of Smallness

Increasingly more and more data fits in smaller storage devices and that creates more challenges for companies. Employees can use USB devices or send large volumes of company information out of the company in email. While many companies have addressed these issues by prohibiting USB devices or using data loss prevention (DLP) technology to limit what can leave the network, the ability to compress data and to store more and more information in smaller and smaller places will remain an issue.

Encryption Policies Abound, Encryption Use Is Sorely Lacking

Most companies have policies that require encryption of company trade secret information and protection of any confidential

---

1. Randolph Kahn, *Economic Espionage in 2017 and Beyond: 10 Shocking Ways They Are Stealing Your Intellectual Property and Corporate Mojo*, Business Law Today (May 30, 2017), https://businesslawtoday.org/2017/05/economic-espionage-in-2017-and-beyond-10-shocking-ways-they-are-stealing-your-intellectual-property-and-corporate-mojo/.

2. *Espionage as a Service: A Means to Instigate Economic Espionage*, Trend Micro (Nov. 28, 2016), https://www.trendmicro.com/vinfo/mx/security/news/cybercrime-and-digital-threats/espionage-as-a-service-a-means-to-instigate-economic-espionage.

> The Chinese electronics giant Huawei offered bonuses to its employees for stealing confidential information from outside companies, according to an indictment of the company on fraud charges issued Monday by the U.S. Department of Justice.[3]

information during transmission. Too often, however, information travels freely without any protection or encryption outside the company: policies are not followed, with potentially significant consequences for the company.

How Some Business Partners Are Legally Mandating the Frustration of Your Information Security Controls

Some countries gain access to others' IP by requiring the transfer of a foreign company's information (i.e., trade secrets), including computer code, as a condition of doing business in the country. Indeed, some countries even legislate the result, according to the World Economic Forum, which stated that "China, for instance, has joined Russia in tightening the requirements placed on foreign companies to store information within national borders."[4]

IP and computer code can also be extracted by providing access to backdoors to encryption technology. In other words, the locked door protecting your trade secrets is now unlocked. From the hearing before the U.S.-China Economic and Security Review Commission:

---

3. Nick Bastone, *Chinese Electronics Giant Huawei Allegedly Offered Bonuses to Any Employee Who Stole Trade Secrets*, Business Insider (Jan. 28, 2019), https://www.businessinsider.com/huawei-indictment-trade-secrets-2019-1.

4. John P. Drzik, *Weaponized AI, Digital Espionage and Other Technology Risks for 2017*, World Economic Forum (Jan. 11, 2017), https://www.weforum.org/agenda/2017/01/technology-risks-amplified-by-global-tensions/.

Recently the government in Beijing has proposed a series of regulatory provisions that would require U.S. tech companies and their foreign customers, especially financial institutions and banks, to turn over source code and encryption software, effectively creating backdoor entry points into otherwise secure networks, all being done, of course, under the guise of cybersecurity.[5]

Executives should be hesitant to sacrifice their company's secret sauce, and lawyers must advise their clients on how to proceed, if at all, with maximum protections in place.

Exploiting Your Relationships and Joint Ventures

"During negotiations between Westinghouse Electric and a Chinese state-owned nuclear power company, the companies began to cooperate more closely and the Chinese partner 'stole from Westinghouse's computers, among other things, proprietary and confidential technical and design specifications for pipes, pipe supports, and pipe routing within the nuclear power plants that Westinghouse was contracted to build, as well as internal Westinghouse communications concerning the company's strategy for doing business,' according to the Wang Dong Indictment."[6]

There have been many cases where a partner is manufacturing in China and uses the U.S. company's molds or designs. If there is no agreement governing the molds or designs and what happens when the relationship ends, then it is quite possible that the Chinese partner will retain the molds or designs for their own benefit. Even if you

---

5. Commercial Cyber Espionage and Barriers to Digital Trade in China, https://www.uscc.gov/sites/default/files/transcripts/June%2015%202015%20Hearing%20Transcript.pdf.

6. Randolph A. Kahn, *Economic Espionage in 2017 and Beyond: 10 Shocking Ways They Are Stealing Your Intellectual Property and Corporate Mojo*, Business Law Today (May 18, 2017), https://www.americanbar.org/groups/business_law/publications/blt/2017/05/05_kahn/.

have an agreement governing what happens when the relationship is over, they may still steal your molds and designs to work against you.

> We believe that data is the phenomenon of our time. It is the world's new natural resource. It is the new basis of competitive advantage, and it is transforming every profession and industry. If all of this is true—even inevitable—then cyber crime, by definition, is the greatest threat to every profession, every industry, every company in the world.
> —Ginny Rometty, IBM CEO[7]

Manage Credentials and Bolster Security

The U.S. Office of Personnel Management (OPM) hack in 2015 and so many others were successful because proper authentication to gain access is not effectuated. Many hackers are successful because IT security is unimpressive at best. That is the reality in part because there is a misunderstanding of how to keep hackers away from your data, as well as a lack of vigilance in doing it. Companies are well served to control credentials more aggressively, increase the authentication levels to access company information, and to revisit their information security policies to determine if security directives are sufficiently clear and sufficiently robust to protect the organization.

- *One-factor* authentication is a unique something the employee knows, such as a strong password.
- *Two-factor* authentication is the first factor plus something the employee possesses, such as a company ID card and security code, a security fob that generates a unique code, etc.
- *Three-factor* authentication adds to the above something the employee is, such as a voice scan, fingerprint, eye scan, etc.

---

7. Sofia Said Birch, IBM's CEO on Hackers, "Cyber Crime Is the Greatest Threat to Every Company in the World," IBM Digital Nordic (Nov. 26, 2015), https://www.ibm.com/blogs/nordic-msp/ibms-ceo-on-hackers-cyber-crime-is-the-greatest-threat-to-every-company-in-the-world/.

The Attacks Grow in Sophistication

Attacks on the information security infrastructure of most companies are getting more sophisticated, more targeted, and more difficult to defend against.

Cyber thieves are using more sophisticated ways to breach company security, including spear-phishing (and their more targeted progeny), zero-day malware attacks, and various types of distributed denial of service assaults. Phishing is now an old-fashioned type of email assault and has been replaced by more sophisticated assaults.

Ransomware is an example of a more sophisticated and potentially damaging attack. It is a special type of malware that secretly installs on a computer and then either holds data hostage or acts as a sophisticated leakware that threatens to publish the data. It works by locking the system and even encrypting the files until ransom is paid.

> Using the intel gathered during reconnaissance, the attackers typically send contextually relevant malware-laden spear-phishing emails to the chosen high-ranking corporate official. This helps ensure they get the credentials with the highest level of access required to infiltrate systems where company crown jewels are stored. Network command and control (C&C) is then established aided by backdoors, remote access Trojans (RATs), or other malware. Attackers then move laterally across the network to seek out top-secret data. The data is then exfiltrated to a site that only the attackers have access to for selling to the highest bidders or delivery to the individual or company that hired them.[8]

---

8. *Espionage as a Service: A Means to Instigate Economic Espionage*, Trend Micro (Nov. 28, 2016), https://www.trendmicro.com/vinfo/mx/security/news/cybercrime-and-digital-threats/espionage-as-a-service-a-means-to-instigate-economic-espionage.

Finding the Cyber Hackers inside Your Environment Can Be Difficult

The hack of OPM, which has been linked to China, is a perfect example of breaching security and trolling for information. In that case, the bad guys made off with the most extensive collection of personal information about U.S. government employees, past and present, ever.

The OPM IT security team had watched the bad guys moving throughout their IT systems for months before the information was extracted. If more timely action had been taken, they likely would have been able to protect the trove of information that was ultimately stolen.[9]

An Avoidable Ransomware Attack

The WannaCry worldwide cyberattack targeted computers beginning on May 12, 2017. It gained entry to computers running older versions of Windows by using an exploit actually developed by the U.S. National Security Agency.

It infected over 200,000 computers in 150 countries, encrypting hard drives and demanding payment in Bitcoin as ransom to decrypt.

Many victims, including the UK's National Health Service, had not widely run software patches issued by Microsoft to close the exploit.[10]

---

9. *See* Committee on Oversight and Government Reform, U.S. House of Representatives, "The OPM Data Breach: How the Government Jeopardized Our National Security for More than a Generation" (Sep. 7, 2016), https://republicans-oversight.house.gov/wp-content/uploads/2016/09/The-OPM-Data-Breach-How-the-Government-Jeopardized-Our-National-Security-for-More-than-a-Generation.pdf.

10. Josh Fruhlinger, "What Is WannaCry Ransomware, How Does It Infect, and Who Was Responsible?," CSO (Aug. 30, 2018), https://www.csoonline.com/article/3227906/what-is-wannacry-ransomware-how-does-it-infect-and-who-was-responsible.html.

Assuming the bad guys will get in from time to time, it is worthwhile walling off data and setting up honey pots in your archives. Honey pots are troves of fictional information marked with titles like "M&A targets" or "products specs" to attract the criminals to a specific location. That misinformation sends the bad guys in the wrong direction.

Lawyers can help customize the honey pots to deal with the various possible assaults on select pools of data, depending upon the source country of the thieves. Thieves in certain countries are known to be after money and pricing information, while others are after M&A targets and product designs.

The Weakest Link May Be Members of Your Workforce or Your Recruiter

IP is being stolen by competitors or by foreign entities hiring operatives who may work at your business for years or even decades. Monitoring and auditing information transmissions and extreme vetting of potential employees must be utilized to mitigate this risk.

Even more troubling is the recent revelation that the Chinese government has sponsored U.S.-based recruitment and headhunting firms that appear perfectly legitimate, but are meant to place operatives at U.S. businesses that have IP deemed strategically important to China. Further, according to the FBI, job advertisements are posted online by those intent on stealing IP to attract employees.

Business Implications

Executives and the Board Must Be Involved

In the last few years, more has been asked of executives and boards of directors to ensure that they are better able to shepherd a company through complex information challenges. Bills have been advanced in Congress to improve the information security knowledge of board members. The Cybersecurity Disclosure Act of 2018, for example, was intended to ensure that someone on a company's board has IT or information security expertise as such problems can and do have a material impact on the company financials. While that particular

> Cybersecurity Disclosure Act of 2019 (Sec. 14C.), states in pertinent part:
>
> (1) to disclose whether any member of the governing body, such as the board of directors or general partner, of the reporting company has expertise or experience in cybersecurity and in such detail as necessary to fully describe the nature of the expertise or experience; and
>
> (2) if no member of the governing body of the reporting company has expertise or experience in cybersecurity, to describe what other aspects of the reporting company's cybersecurity were taken into account by any person, such as an official serving on a nominating committee, that is responsible for identifying and evaluating nominees for membership to the governing body.

bill was not signed into law, executives and boards should expect to see more bills like it in the near future. At the time of this writing, the 2019 bill was introduced in Senate. Serious consideration should be given to having such expertise on the board.

Is a Data Breach Inevitable?

We see an endless parade of headlines announcing the hacking of well-known companies where critical information was misappropriated. Can a disaster be averted?

Companies are under assault every day, all day long, in various ways. While best-of-breed information security technology will help keep the bad guys out, it almost seems inevitable that, eventually, someone will get in and cause trouble for your business. So what practical steps can executives and boards take to preempt or at least prepare for a bad event?

- Build a SWAT team that will deal with intrusions. At a minimum the team should include IT, information security professionals, legal, and external communications.

- Make reasonable efforts to secure the IT environment.
- Train, train, and train. People are the weak link, so get them to make information security a way of life.
- Communicate the importance of protecting information and what the employee's role is in protecting it.
- Conduct tabletop cyberattack exercises at all levels in the company.
- Seriously consider buying cyber insurance.
- Conduct periodic risk assessments.

The Need to Share to Win

Companies don't like to talk about getting hacked and having their information stolen, and for good reason. It draws negative attention

> A previously unnamed U.S. energy company that agreed to a record $2.7 million settlement after it left 30,000 records about its information security assets exposed online for 70 days in violation of energy sector cybersecurity regulations has been named as California utility PG&E.[11]

from customers, media, and regulators. After all, IT security failures raise questions about management doing its job or IT leadership failing to keep the bad guys out, but it also tells other bad guys about inadequate security, which could invite further cyberattacks.

On December 18, 2015, the Cyber Information Sharing Act became law. The law was designed to create a voluntary cybersecurity information sharing process to encourage public and private entities to share cyber threat information while protecting classified information, intelligence sources, privacy, and more. Seriously consider sharing and learning from assaults, attacks, and the failures of others.

---

11. Mathew J. Schwartz, *Breach Reveal: PG&E Exposed 30,000 Sensitive Records*, Bank Info Security (Aug. 28, 2018), https://www.bankinfosecurity.com/breach-reveal-pge-exposed-30000-sensitive-records-a-11429

Perform a Risk Assessment

When your corporate IP may be in jeopardy, it's prudent to assess risk and mitigate the issues that create the greatest risk. For example, if your organization hires IT personnel from abroad, then it is essential to perform deep background checks. If your organization hires from countries that are at issue, then you may want to refrain from hiring from such countries. If you are moving data to the cloud, then select secure and functionality-rich providers. If third parties have access to company data, then assess their information management practices and mitigate deficiencies. To properly assess risk, companies should methodically assess risks and develop a roadmap to mitigate them.

Some Technologies Make Protecting Information Tougher

Social media, communications technologies, the IoT, and other newer technologies that promote connectivity to the internet and collect and transmit information—sometimes without your knowledge—pose a more challenging risk. While promoting connectivity and accessibility, they may provide only limited security and make information more vulnerable to cyberattacks. With predictions of greater use and reliance on these technologies going forward, greater vigilance through training and audit may help limit theft of trade secrets.

Volumes Make Stealing Your Business Way Easier

Technology and vigilance can limit exfiltration of large volumes of company data through the internet. Approaches include limiting where information can be stored, preempting the use of certain technologies, limiting the use of USB devices, controlling wireless access, limiting where certain classes of data can be stored, and disposing of data when it is no longer needed.

Classify information in order to properly protect it, including trade secrets and private information. Classification helps deal with the reality that not all information is equal in value and therefore, allows for greater time and effort to be spent protecting the more valuable data. After all, organizations don't generally have the money or personnel to babysit all of their information 24/7. Therefore, if you have classifications regimes that work, use them. If you don't, then create them.

Encrypt Early and Often

Most companies have policies that require encryption of company trade secret information and protection of any confidential information sent outside the company. But too often, information travels freely without any protection or encryption outside the company. Organizations should make sure encryption technology is available and being used.

Defensibly Dispose of Outdated Information

It's axiomatic that the bigger the information pile, the bigger the information security risk. Therefore, it stands to reason that organizations must make an effort to cull information that is no longer needed. Properly disposing of outdated and unnecessary information promotes business efficiency, reduces storage costs, mitigates privacy and information security risks, and reduces costs of discovery. Making the pile smaller demands that content be disposed of when law and policy allow. Remember that when cleaning up any information pile, the company's records retention schedule must be considered and any information needed for an audit, litigation, or investigation must be preserved.

Legal Implications

Think about Security at the Contract Level

In addition to state actors, sophisticated cyber mercenaries are now increasingly the parties stealing IP. Lawyers can help address the new threats by ensuring that heightened security functionality is part of new technology purchases when negotiating contracts on behalf of their company, mandating that company information is stored only in hyper-secure, compliance-driven clouds, and that policy dictates that information is encrypted when "in flight" or "at rest."

In relationships where partners conduct business globally, it is essential for local lawyers to be engaged in order to help navigate local law. Equally as important is limiting access to trade secrets and IP that are not part of the transactions. That may mean limiting access to facilities and systems where such information is housed, and having strict rules ironed out about who gets access to what information. If collaboration tools are used to work on the partnership, enacting strict rules about what can and cannot be stored and shared in such environments is essential.

Make sure that your IP is secured wherever you do business. If you must bring your IP to contractual relationships in other jurisdictions, make sure there are agreements in place for every reasonable eventuality, understanding that such measures still may not offer enough protection when doing business with some countries or partners that are determined to steal your IP. Knowing this reality, companies should mitigate by implementing a variety of measures beyond contracts to protect their information and IP, including knowing where IP is stored, implementing data loss prevention tools, disaggregating processes, and limiting access to IP.

Think about Security at the Policy Level

Policies tell your employees what is expected of them and tells the outside world you care enough about a topic to seek to regulate it. Being able to take action against employees misappropriating company information, including IP and trade secrets, starts with clear policies prohibiting theft. But having clear policies will only help when dealing with employees or insiders who steal; it won't be effective in deterring a state actor or cybercriminals.

Think about Security at the Compliance Methodology Level

Lawyers can help IT professionals combat persistent threats against a company's information. Compliance methodology should be applied to information security practices, helping systematize rigor and diligence in the process. Compliance methodology tends to institutionalize vigilance and good corporate behavior. Following the methodology helps the company and its employees get it right and helps insulate the company when there is a failure, as the built-in rigor manifests reasonableness. In other words, it is important to demonstrate that the company cares about doing the right thing, which matters to shareholders, markets, the court of public opinion, courts, regulators, and the bottom line.

Think about Security at the Business Process Level

To address protecting company information, start with knowing what information deserves protection, what business creates or manages the information, and where it is stored. Large companies usually have information security classification regimes that are underutilized or improperly utilized by employees, and technology that can apply the rules automatically is too often not harnessed either. As a general rule, taking reasonable precautions to protect your information allows you to assert your legal rights. For example, protecting information and IP, by classifying trade secrets as trade secrets and labeling them as such.

Lawyers can help reinvigorate classification regimes, simplify and redraft existing classification policies, and insist on the use of encryption technology. Once again, compliance methodology can help institutionalize vigilance.[12]

---

12. Randolph A. Kahn, *Economic Espionage in 2017 and Beyond: 10 Shocking Ways They Are Stealing Your Intellectual Property and Corporate Mojo*, Business Law Today (May 18, 2017), https://www.americanbar.org/groups/business_law/publications/blt/2017/05/05_kahn/.

Rule 16

Introduce Transparency into Your Information Sources

Executive Takeaway

With information growing at mind-numbing speed, companies must build a culture of transparency with tools, people, and processes to exploit the full value of their information.

Background

We have learned in the last few decades that it is very easy to create information and it is very easy for the information creator to find value in that information immediately. But timely access to information and the value it adds can be elusive. Typically, there are no rules on where unstructured information must reside, so creators and recipients store it wherever they find it convenient, minimizing its utility to other business units or employees. As information grows, the challenge is to know what information you have, have it provided to users in a digestible form, and make it available for decision making and the running of your business. Building or buying technology and developing policies that promote transparency and having the right eyes on the right data is essential in 2020.

Data Visualization

Generally, employees are better able to analyze and use data when it is presented in an easy-to-digest form, often using visual tools

> The VP of marketing at a major technology company is trying to determine if its marketing efforts are providing the biggest bang for each marketing buck spent. With so many initiatives underway across the globe it's hard to determine exactly how much is being spent to build a pipeline of new business and whether the type of marketing activity is making economic sense. A marketing dashboard may be useful to address the various issues confounding our marketing executive to provide a composite view of all of the relevant data about the company's various marketing activities. It would provide a quick view that quantifies the overall impact of marketing efforts: what is being spent to acquire new customers and whether such efforts are positively impacting sales among other important insights. It allows management to see high-level statistics or a consolidated view of all activities across the enterprise and then to dig deeper if need be. It would provide a mechanism to evaluate different types of marketing activities to see which builds the customer pipeline more cost effectively.

such as pictorials, graphs, charts, and dashboards. While companies have been aggregating data in various forms for decades and using various kinds of dashboard and other tools to present the right data, to the right people, at the right time to do their job, that task gets harder as information grows, especially if it is poorly managed. Similarly, as volumes have grown over time, so to have storage locations. This further compounds the problem of making data meaningful as sources are not easily integrated. For a company to be "faster, better, cheaper," it is imperative that they find the right tools and processes to provide visual data to the right recipient, whether that recipient is a line worker or an executive. Information is more valuable when the recipient can quickly digest it and take action. For example, data visualization can be used to improve business processes, identify product failures, or predict sales volumes by region, state, or county.

Dashboards Help Decision-Making Effectiveness
Here are their benefits:

- Dashboards can consolidate data from other operational systems that presently don't communicate with each other.
- A dashboard, if created properly for operations, sales and other functions, can be a one-time expense, unless or until you choose to tweak it.
- *Dashboards can actually save money,* reducing the need for internal staff to be creating and monitoring costly reports.
- Perhaps most important, *dashboards provide fact-based, real-time data*—limited in quantity and quality only by your customization—that support timely and well-informed decision making.[1]

Customer Experience

Intuitive customer interaction with the company through communications tools, including websites for tracking transactions and delivery statuses, smooths the buying experience for the customer, minimizes cost in the company's responses to customers, and can create a stickiness between the customer and company. If the information customers want is readily available and they feel like the company is taking care of their needs, delivering on time, and honest about its offerings, then the freer flow of information tends to inspire loyalty. Things like order tracking, providing end of year 1099 tax documents, printing return labels, and checking on product status all tend to advance the

> Gamification is a way to motivate employees and others to do some activity or learn some task in a non-gaming context with rewards that are like playing a game. Gamification can be used for all kinds of business activities, training, marketing, sales, and even getting employees, including executives, to better secure the company information.

---

1. Matt Crum, *Using a Dashboard to Improve Decision Making Effectiveness*, FrankCrum (Apr. 12, 2016), https://blog.frankcrum.com/using-a-dashboard-to-improve-decision-making-effectiveness.

customer's experience with your company and minimize cost for the company to respond or address the customer's concerns. Information exists and smart companies are finding ways to put more and more of the information in the hands of the customers to empower them and build relationships. Of course, companies can't and won't put everything online, but executives need to make decisions about what should go online, as it may advance and promote customer loyalty. However, the opposite can be true too: if delivery times are a problem, the company would be penalized by making such information available to the customer and it may damage the relationship.

Chatbots Are Getting More Intelligent

As interactive voice response did twenty years ago in promoting customer service through the telephone, chatbots (virtual assistant computer programs designed to simulate conversation with human users) are answering customer questions and addressing needs and issues without human intervention. As these tools continue to evolve, they address more and more business issues that will augment customer service and minimize cost.

> Darcy happened to be a former computer programmer, so she was able to dream up a very unusual solution to this problem: Woebot, a text-chatbot therapist. Working with a team of psychologists and Andrew Ng, a pioneer in artificial intelligence, Darcy wrote a set of conversational prompts that walks users through the practice of C.B.T. In a chipper style, the bot helps users challenge their "distorted thinking"; it coaxes users to describe their moods more clearly. Since Woebot is just software, it could be made freely available worldwide, and it could, in Silicon Valley terms, "scale"—or converse with thousands of people simultaneously. It could check in and nudge users with superhuman diligence; it would be available at all hours. "Woebot can be there at 2 a.m. if you're having a panic attack and no therapist can, or should be, in bed with you," Darcy says.[2]

---

2. Clive Thompson, *May A.I. Help You?*, New York Times (Nov. 14, 2018), https://www.nytimes.com/interactive/2018/11/14/magazine/tech-design-ai-chatbot.html.

Location-Based Business

Increasingly, companies are connecting their computing environments with customers and other potential end users for their services and using products that create connections, maximizing purchases and minimizing the cost of customer acquisition. A business could tell a purchaser of a new product that it has been delivered to a particular store or that a product that was out has now been restocked. By having the connection between company and customer, there can be transparency into services and offerings at the point when and where they are available.

> The Lowe's Vision: In-Store Navigation app is the latest advancement from Lowe's Innovation Labs, the retailer's disruptive innovation hub. The Labs are focused on creating new solutions to enhance the retail experience for customers and employees.
>
> "Our research shows that helping make it easier for customers to find products in stores not only makes for a better shopping experience, it allows our associates to spend more time advising on home improvement projects," said Kyle Nel, executive director of Lowe's Innovation Labs. "With Lowe's Vision: In-Store Navigation, we've created a more seamless experience using breakthrough technology so customers can save time shopping and focus more on their project."
>
> Lowe's Vision: In-Store Navigation uses Tango-enabled motion tracking, area learning and depth perception to guide customers through the store using a mixed reality interface. When a customer comes to Lowe's to get started on a project, they can use any Tango-enabled smartphone to create a list of their required items in the app and access product reviews and information to make an informed decision. From there, directional prompts overlaid onto the real-world setting guide the customer to each item using the most efficient route around the store.

Lowe's first partnered with Tango to introduce Lowe's Vision, one of the first apps to leverage the Tango platform. Bringing spatial perception to the smartphone, Lowe's Vision acts as a "digital power tool" for customers embarking on a home improvement project. The technology enables the user to measure spaces and visualize how products like appliances and home décor will look in their home. Lowe's Vision and Lowe's Vision: In-Store Navigation technologies are significant developments in Lowe's efforts to build a portfolio of augmented reality offerings that meet the needs of the evolving customer.[3]

Business Implications

Transparency Culture

Executives need to nurture their organizations to move away from hiding data to being more transparent where appropriate. Information is an important part of competitive advantage. By creating a transparent information connection, companies can increase a deeper customer relationship, promote sales, minimize the costs of customer acquisition, and improve customer service.

Everyone in the organization should have the responsibility to find ways to capitalize on making information transparent. The finance guy should allow the quality guy to see financials that help his business unit understand the long-term costs related to quality defects. The warehouse manager should allow the customer service team to access data that can provide real-time tracking of shipping to customers. Scrutiny invites improvement.

---

3. *Lowe's Introduces In-Store Navigation Using Augmented Reality*, PR Newswire: Lowe's (Mar. 23, 2017), https://www.prnewswire.com/news-releases/lowes-introduces-in-store-navigation-using-augmented-reality-300428415.html.

RULE 16: INTRODUCE TRANSPARENCY INTO YOUR INFORMATION SOURCES

Customer and Company Stickiness

Stickiness evolves from loyalty, loyalty evolves from transparency, and information is the connective tissue that links your business to its customer. People believe companies to be more honest and trustworthy if they are openly sharing information related to the services and products they desire.

End User Interface

Businesses that provide better optics into their service offerings and products through easier-to-navigate websites and other tools tend to promote deeper, more productive relationships with customers, making the inventory less mysterious and promoting sales.

Why the User Interface Matters

User interface (sometimes referred to as GUI: graphical user interface) is the way a customer interacts with a company through a system, such as their website. That physical layout and look and

---

> According to our social media statistics roundup, about 42 percent of customers use social media to voice their frustrations. On the contrary, customers are also likely to advocate for brands on social media. This mix of emotions toward brands is what we call sentiment.
>
> Social sentiment is how social media users feel about a particular brand. This sentiment is typically tracked with scraping technologies and interpreted using natural language processing.
>
> Positive, negative, and even neutral sentiment can hold a lot of insight for businesses that consider social media as a key part of its marketing strategy. To study sentiment, we need to understand how it's analyzed and the different ways it's applied.[4]

---

4. Elena Vinokurtseva, *What Is Sentiment Analysis and How Is It Used in Social Media?*, G2 Crowd (Feb. 22, 2019), https://learn.g2crowd.com/sentiment-analysis.

feel have become critically important. User experience (UX) is a constantly evolving art and science, presenting information and opportunities in ways that allow for thorough analysis and quicker decision making. To the user, the interface *is* the system. When an interface is not intuitive, productivity and confidence in processes are reduced. UI and UX designers don't just put a pretty picture on a piece of software. They can make or break it. By enhancing the customer experience, customers interact easier, stay longer, have better sense of your inventory and buy more. For lawyers, it is important to remember that the various physical layouts that customers see may have legal significance and may be relevant in the context of discovery. For example, the privacy statement displayed in a 5-point font or the terms hidden in an out-of-the-way page could be called out as unreasonable.

Legal Implications

Companies Remain Responsible for What Their Smart Technology Does

As user interfaces become smarter they tend to make decisions autonomously or semi-autonomously and that may have business or legal implications. In that regard, the ways in which customers or the buying public interface with the company should be managed as companies will be responsible for the actions of their technology.

> Using Facebook's AI-driven, self-service platform to purchase ads, companies and brands can target their message to different demographics. In September [2017], ProPublica reported that some of those demographics include those with racist or anti-Semitic views. Facebook said those categories were created by an algorithm, not a human, and removed them as an option.[5]

---

5. Olivia Krauth, *Artificial Ignorance: The 10 Biggest AI Failures of 2017*, TechRepublic (Jan. 4, 2018), https://www.techrepublic.com/article/the-10-biggest-ai-failures-of-2017/.

Policies, Laws, Rules Still Apply

When using smarter technologies including smarter interfaces that make decisions on their own, it is important for lawyers and business folks to proactively figure out how to manage the informational output of the systems. New policies and new controls may be needed to manage not only the system but the informational output. Whether the company is capturing personal information transmitted by a chatbot or extracting information provided to a website, company policies, laws, and regulations may all apply. Similarly, if information is potentially relevant to a lawsuit, discovery rules may also apply. But the problem is that managing this information output can be way more complex based on how the systems are structured.

Transparency for Law Department Efficiency

While law departments have been managing budgets and comparing efficacy of outside law firms for years, new technologies help analyze the data in greater granularity to provide more efficient and economical legal services. Having greater transparency into information that runs the law department can have a significant bottom line impact and also better results from legal spend. For example, analyzing costs associated with similar types of cases but handled by different outside law firms to compare cost-effective representation. In other words, make sure the company is making the best use of its law department budget but also getting good quality representation from the most economical firms.

Rule 17

Manage the Expanding IoT Data Universe

Executive Takeaway

The rapidly growing Internet of Things can produce value, but also carries risks.

Background

The Internet of Things (IoT) includes various kinds of devices that have internet connectivity and the capacity to collect and transmit information through hardware, such as sensors, cameras, recorders, and other non-typical computing devices. To understand the information flow in the IoT world is to understand the goals of the entity implementing the device. The end user company purchaser may be using that device for one purpose and the manufacturer of the device may be getting information or insight about its use from a different perspective.

For example, a company implements a new health awareness program and decides to give each employee a wearable health device to promote a healthier lifestyle. However, the program is motivated by the desire to reduce insurance premiums and medical expenses. In this situation, four parties may be getting information—the employee wearing the device, the company that issued the device, the insurance company, and the wearable manufacturer. Each party's interest in the information may be different and the value of the

> Global IoT market potential growth rates CAGR of 21 percent by 2026.[1]

information certainly reflects that. The end user may care that he/she is burning more calories, the company wants to know that everyone is wearing the device, the insurance company wants to know how active each employee is, and the manufacturer wants to know everything. Whoever you are in the IoT information ecosystem you dictate what information you want and what value you will get from it. The selling proposition for the wearable device is about a healthy employee. However, for the manufacturer of the device, it may initially be about the sale of the device but ultimately about the informational output from the device that can be repackaged, reused, and sold as a new revenue stream.

IoT devices, some of which have been around for years (pacemakers, home security systems, automobile safety sensors) have the capability to create and transmit information, often without any real notice to the user.

Where It's Hot

The availability of connected sensors allows us to monitor bridges, pipelines, and other infrastructure, allowing focused, preemptive maintenance. Why visit the pipeline when the pipeline can talk to you in real time? More than just a byproduct of a mechanical process, the information created by this massive number of devices is valuable in that it can be used to interact with other devices, predict and fix failures, and perform these tasks independently.

---

1. https://www.marketwatch.com/press-release/cagr-of-21-internet-of-things-iot-market-potential-growth-with-cagr-of-21-by-2026.

IoT is changing the business landscape in substantial ways, such as sensors and devices that:

- Collect information on human activity, body functions, and medical issues.
- Make autonomous vehicles a possibility.
- Make cities smart by re-routing traffic, monitoring pollution and crime, and notifying maintenance professionals of mechanical failures.
- Help us in our home by managing energy use and efficiency, shopping online, or automatically vacuuming our carpets.
- Monitor manufacturing activities to detect poorly manufactured parts, address bottlenecks in assembly lines, monitoring atmospheric conditions to ensure product finishes will adhere properly, and assessing what component parts need maintenance.
- Monitor and adjust aviation controls including fuel efficiency, maintenance, and servicing malfunctioning parts.
- Monitor rail system conditions to predict landslides and flooding.

> As the local gas company came into the twenty-first century, it transformed its business from being largely reliant on "dumb" devices and a complaint from the public to inform the company that services was interrupted, for example. With the application of "smart" devices, the gas company now knows just about everything about their energy delivery system without much if any human intervention. It knows when demands are overburdening a sector of its distribution network and why. It knows when a gas line is leaking and where it is located. It knows if key components of the system are about to fail and may even automatically order a replacement part without the involvement of a person. This new smarter system is hugely valuable to their business in so many ways. But each of the smart devices collects data whether you know it or not. And this new monster body of data has emerged in most businesses where none of it existed a few short years ago with little thought or planning about who owns it, where its stored, who has the right to use it, and how well its protected. For most executives or even the employees of your company IoT data can fall into the category of "out of sight, out of mind." Until a breach or nonconsensual use of personal data makes it all too visible.

But Security Remains a Major Issue

The merits of IoT are apparent on its face but the connected world creates risks and concerns for any IoT device or process. It is easy to envision an interconnected IoT world where companies rely upon various kinds of devices to run their operations and processes or provide services or products more efficiently. However, as the connected world is now seeing, IoT risks are abundant and growing. The devices are usually not as secure as other technology devices within the enterprise and all of these devices are unleashed on the internet with all their risks and imperfections. As with many aspects of your information universe, this area requires weighing the opportunities against the risks and mitigating the potential thefts.

Smart control valves in a petroleum line help control use, flow, maintenance, and security but because they are connected to the internet there are inherent risks associated with their use. Similarly, when Tesla remotely unlocked unused battery capacity to allow vehicles to drive farther during Hurricane Florence, those connections to the internet created new and additional potential security risks for the driver and Tesla.

Remote access and monitoring of environmental and security systems means that homeowners have more control over their living space, but the risk is that the same access is a window into the space for use by malicious actors. Devices on the internet are getting even more connected. Programs like IFTTT (If This, Then That) help users leverage the interfaces between devices so that they can easily, say, pause a robotic vacuum cleaner automatically while the cell phone is ringing. What that means in practical terms is that with more connected systems comes more potential exposure.

BUSINESS IMPLICATIONS

Unintentional and Potentially Valuable Data

The information harvested and processed by devices provides a wealth of insight about your customers, suppliers, and competitors. While removing friction from processes, removing human error, removing delay, making the availability of useful information timelier is important, it is just as important to see the information itself as something that can be combined, processed, and transformed into something even more valuable. At the same time, it is critically important to understand the risks to customers, suppliers, competitive advantage and, in some cases, national security, if IoT is not handled properly.

Increasingly, organizations that rely on IoT devices are creating a large volume of unintended data, which is a valuable byproduct of IoT devices that is generally hidden from company employees. As IoT devices create information and automatically move it to some third-party repository, companies need to understand who owns that information, who has use of that information, and who is managing that information up front before implementing IoT devices.

Depending upon how IoT devices are used, their information byproduct may provide insights on how productive employees are, how the factory and its component parts are functioning, how customers are utilizing your products, or whether or not you're wasting resources, among a myriad of other things.

> The continued growth of the IoT industry is going to be a transformative force across all organizations. By integrating all of our modern day devices with internet connectivity, the IoT market is on pace to grow to over $3 trillion annually by 2026.
>
> We forecast that there will be more than 64 billion IoT devices by 2025, up from about 10 billion in 2018.[2]

---

2. Peter Newman, *IoT Report: How Internet of Things Technology Growth Is Reaching Mainstream Companies and Consumers*, Business Insider (Jan. 28, 2019), https://www.businessinsider.com/internet-of-things-report.

Legal Implications

Protect Privacy

Connected devices can monitor the environment and help us see our cities in a holistic way. The costs of increasing infrastructure capacity—from water pipes to highways—can be minimized when these resources are utilized more efficiently. The use of this type of smart city technology can improve lives of individuals but can also start to feel like Big Brother as governmental agencies know more about its citizens, and their actions and whereabouts.

Devices connecting employees and devices connecting customers provide a whole host of potential informational benefits, but also risk impacting privacy. While data from devices extracted from the chest of patients may provide insight into how the product is functioning, or whether the patient is rejecting the device, there is the risk that the company now possesses personal health information, which carries with it legal obligations and information security challenges that must be addressed proactively.

Laws Are Evolving to Address Connected Devices

California Senate Bill 327 on connected devices goes into effect January 1, 2020—the same day that the new California privacy (CPPA) law goes into effect.

> Existing law requires a business to take all reasonable steps to dispose of customer records within its custody or control containing personal information when the records are no longer to be retained by the business by shredding, erasing, or otherwise modifying the personal information in those records to make it unreadable or undecipherable. Existing law also requires a business that owns, licenses, or maintains personal information about a California resident to implement and maintain reasonable security procedures and practices appropriate to the nature of the information, to protect the personal information from

unauthorized access, destruction, use, modification, or disclosure. Existing law authorizes a customer injured by a violation of these provisions to institute a civil action to recover damages.

This bill, beginning on January 1, 2020, would require a manufacturer of a connected device, as those terms are defined, to equip the device with a reasonable security feature or features that are appropriate to the nature and function of the device, appropriate to the information it may collect, contain, or transmit, and designed to protect the device and any information contained therein from unauthorized access, destruction, use, modification, or disclosure, as specified.[3]

Conflicting Laws

Companies collecting IoT data should ensure contractual rights to collect the data, and that the contract dictates what they are able to do or not do with the data. Further, companies should consult their lawyers regarding captured IoT data and whether or not it conflicts with other laws including, for example, the Electronic Communications Privacy Act and Stored Communications Act.

The E-Discovery Problem

Data related to IoT devices can be stored on the devices themselves, in a cloud service, on related devices, or somewhere on the internet. IoT will further complicate e-discovery going forward. Companies should proactively inventory sources of IoT data and have a plan in place to preserve, collect, and produce such data if needed in the context of a lawsuit or other formal matter.

---

3. U.S.C. § 1 (Title 1.81.26). [https://leginfo.legislature.ca.gov/faces/billTextClient.xhtml?bill_id=201720180SB327.]

> ## Lock Down Your Devices!
>
> A botnet is the term used to describe a collection of devices commandeered by hackers to stage an attack. The Mirai botnet gained access to IoT devices, like cameras and other smart devices, by trying 61 frequently used factory-set username/password combinations. During the peak of its activity in September 2016, the Mirai botnet exploited 600,000 IoT devices.
>
> "On October 21, a Mirai attack targeted the popular DNS provider DYN. This event prevented Internet users from accessing many popular websites, including AirBnB, Amazon, Github, HBO, Netflix, Paypal, Reddit, and Twitter, by disturbing the DYN name-resolution service."[4]

---

4. *Inside the Infamous Mirai IoT Botnet: A Retrospective Analysis*, Cloudflare (Dec. 14, 2017), https://blog.cloudflare.com/inside-mirai-the-infamous-iot-botnet-a-retrospective-analysis/.

Rule 18

The Rule of Yes

The customer, culture, and employees along with business continuity must be at the heart of every technology investment.[1]

Executive Takeaway

Say yes to new technologies that improve employee communication, collaboration, and productivity.

Background

Some business executives and legal professionals respond reflexively to what they see as requests for "shiny new technology toys" by the workforce. Their instinct may be to disregard the requests for new things or believe that current technology is sufficient. They may also over-emphasize risk and, in the process, miss opportunities. Before saying no to new technologies, assess the business benefit and seek to mitigate risk. If you don't embrace new technologies, employees may introduce new technologies to work that are not sufficiently vetted and not ready for prime time.

---

1. Daniel Newman, *Top 10 Digital Transformation Trends for 2019*, Forbes (Sep. 11, 2018), https://www.forbes.com/sites/danielnewman/2018/09/11/top-10-digital-transformation-trends-for-2019/#1a07b4de3c30.

Over the last twenty years, employees have been bringing new technologies into their companies because it helps them conduct business more efficiently and effectively. This forces technology departments to either refuse the technology once they find out about its unsanctioned use or forbid its use until the company can perform sufficient diligence to determine if it is secure and meets business needs. Both of those approaches frustrate the employees' ability to use the technology to perform their business function in, perhaps, innovatively productive ways.

Companies should know what is in the marketplace and drive the implementation of new technologies. While such an approach is prudent, what we have learned is that employees have been telling their employers through this act of bringing in technology that the company has not been keeping pace with the technologies that employees like to use or that they are too slow to act, which can be perceived as a no. Certainly, companies should not allow employees to dictate what technology is being used and expose the company to potentially substandard technology from an information security perspective. However, companies are well served to understand what employees are asking for and why.

Bringing In and Keeping the Best and the Brightest

As the workforce ages and retires, a new breed of employee has grown up functioning with different technologies that make them more efficient and productive. To attract those dynamic employees, companies should understand the technologies that drive change in a younger workforce to ensure that the company is giving its new hires the tools to make them most efficient to do their jobs. Email may have been good for twenty years, but recently graduated generations want to communicate in a quicker, less formal manner.

Enhancing Collaboration

As the information pile has grown, finding better ways to share and collaborate has become more difficult. Having more employees working within their own information silos doesn't promote company knowledge sharing and cross-pollination of information for business purposes across lines of business. Collaborative tools, such as Slack, have allowed groups to improve teamwork: having every interaction and file available in one place instead of having to ask one another "do you have that email?" or "where did we store that version?" As a result, Slack, and tools like it, have become mainstream with a loyal base of followers, spurring the creation of a team communication tool category that now includes heavyweights Microsoft (Teams), Facebook (Workplace), and others.

Ten benefits of enhanced collaboration:

1. Promoting an agile company
2. Conducting more productive meetings
3. Connecting remote workers in a disconnected workforce
4. Keeping the group up to speed on what others are doing
5. Helping management keep track of worker productivity
6. Providing clarity on what employees are working on
7. Promoting teamwork
8. Attracting and keeping top-tier employees
9. Speeding up business processes
10. Knowledge sharing for retiring/departing employees

> "When a Pacific Gas and Electric lineman retires, a fair amount of experimental wisdom goes out the company's doors. Without that knowledge, a replacement can swamp a service truck or get shot at by an angry rancher when driving the wrong fire road to get to a faulty substation... To prevent those scenarios and help avoid countless others, Pacific Gas and Electric Corp. of San Francisco have developed a knowledge management strategy aimed at heading off the loss of a significant trove of knowledge packed into the minds of its older baby boomers."[2]

---

2. Jonathan Gourlay, *Knowledge Management Strategy Helps Gas Company Retain Worker Know-How*, TechTarget (Jan. 17, 2013), https://searchcontentmanagement.techtarget.com/feature/Knowledge-management-strategy-helps-gas-company-retain-worker-know-how.

Is Your Knowledge Leaving the Building?

The American workforce is aging. What that means in practical terms is that many of your best and brightest minds will be leaving in the coming years and taking with them a massive body of knowledge about your business and how to make it innovate and hum. Unless you can figure out how to extract that information for the ongoing benefit of your business, it will be gone forever.

Communication Technologies Help Structure Modern Work Life

Over the last couple of decades, companies' workforces have become reliant upon various communications technologies to run their day and work lives. Email, for example, was not only a productive communication tool but also a way for employees to know what needed to get done, the status of projects, who was supposed to take action, and more. Other newer technologies have similarly promoted the

---

Six Simple Steps to Build Your Knowledge-Wrangling Program

1. Determine which employees possess unique knowledge about your business that, if lost, will have a negative impact.
2. Have managers assess their teams regularly so the company can be proactive to capture back some of the knowledge before it's too late.
3. Focus on knowledge that is likely undocumented and special and valuable to the ongoing running of your business.
4. Have each manager assess the importance of employee special knowledge to determine which employees should be focused on before they leave. Not everyone will have important information that can't be gleaned somewhere else or must be recaptured.
5. Harness internal databases and external tools to determine which employees, given tenure and other factors, are likely to retire in the next few years.
6. Once the critical-knowledge employees' identities are determined, the manager and the employee must determine the best way to share that knowledge back to the company.

structuring of employees' workdays and provide other functionality. In other words, it is not just about communicating, it is about making employees productive by giving them a tool that helps them manage the various work tasks.

BUSINESS IMPLICATIONS

When technology makes business sense, employees find value in its use and the legal and compliance issue can be addressed, the company should seriously consider implementation of such technology. In that sense, companies should resist the obstructionist or the purist who doesn't think the technology is a perfect legal or compliance fit for the enterprise.

Saying No All the Time Has Its Consequences

Organizations can block opportunities or innovation or even create an environment that fosters "shadow IT," a wild west of secretly implemented technologies, which could pose even greater risk to the organization. Completely locking down even the most "secure" environments is near impossible in today's interconnected environment.

Technology Adoption Pattern

Technology adoption seems to follow a pattern when new technology is introduced:

1. Someone comes up with a way of doing things that is riskier, or at least seems riskier than the status quo.
2. The new technology is dismissed—usually most vocally by those who have a vested interest in the status quo.
3. And then slowly but surely, the new technology wins over the company management and adds value to the enterprise.

> **Getting to the Rule of Yes**
>
> A large life insurance company presented an example: A veteran executive there knew that the company's workforce was aging and that they needed to attract and retain new talent. The realization emerged that money alone was likely not going to be enough inducement to transform the workforce. Millennials, he found, seemed to need more than a good-paying job. Younger employees, who lived and breathed collaborative technologies and time-saving tools in their personal lives, wanted to work in a way that suited their lifestyle, that allowed them to communicate and collaborate in ways that their parents could never have dreamed of. "And that realization," he said, "got us to the Rule of Yes." "When employees demonstrate through words or actions that new technology may make some business sense," he said, "think long and hard about saying yes." Of course, organizations have to conduct reasonable diligence, but the instinct should no longer be to discard the technology out of hand. Organizations must think about what the intrusion into the company's tech world order means to the organization and why they think that matters. As long as information security and record lifecycle standards can govern the data that belongs to the company, the gains to be made might well be much greater than the perceived risks.

Centralized Vetting to Avoid Duplicative Purchases

There must be a process in place for companies to evaluate collaboration and communication tools in the marketplace to see which are in the best position to address needs across the enterprise. That requires a proactive effort to determine needs in various business units as well as technical and legal needs.

While the company may be better off with the Rule of Yes, centralized vetting of new technologies still needs to take place to ensure all functional business requirements are addressed. By vetting and approving technologies that employees want to use through their vetting process, the company's IT leadership can ensure that the new technology is not exposing the company to unreasonable security risks. Not least by not forcing it underground.

Centralized vetting also helps ensure that the company is not making duplicative purchases or purchasing the same or similar technologies across the company and that buying for the entire company may carry with it cost savings. Let IT recalibrate the evaluation process to focus on where the risks can actually be and not linked to the knee-jerk dismissal of new technology as "not the way we do things here."

Remove Obstacles

Having information is very different from having ready access to the right information to be able to efficiently run your business. Information is what allows all levels of decision-makers to make informed decisions. But as the volume of information has grown exponentially, having the right stuff is no small challenge. Removing unneeded information is a given and is fundamental to any records program. Simplifying processes and removing redundant ones keeps the business from needlessly adding more to the pile, getting in the way of knowledge.

Fund and Support New Information Flows

Information, in all its various forms, is the way business functions, day in and day out. Whether we're talking about communications technologies used to execute a contract, social media that helps market your wares, or structured data being harvested for big data purposes, information is pushed or pulled in all kinds of ways every day to make your business hum. Practically speaking, you may need to fund technology and tools to better manage content in places you never expected to do businesses. Capturing Facebook-focused marketing materials or LinkedIn-focused recruiting efforts for example, will be essential as the law requires your company to retain such information. The regulators don't tell companies how to transact business or what technologies to utilize but they do expect compliance-minded practices to be brought forward into new business processes.

Building Institutional Knowledge When Using Collaboration Technology

While it might be important to know details of the product launched back in 2017 or why a big contract was structured the way it was, what is the best way to make that knowledge available to others in your organization? Often, that type of knowledge is captured in the heads of individuals, in their work computers, or in their workspaces. This unstructured environment traps so much institutional knowledge in the individual employee and in the way they do their job. When using collaboration environments, joint work products and the information artifacts related to them exist beyond the individual person and become part of the information collective.

Legal Implications

There are many collaboration and social tools that make business happen much more efficiently and promote a more productive workforce, but lawyers need to address a series of issues proactively before companies commit to these technologies.

Build Functional Legal and Compliance Requirements into New Technology

Often legal and compliance needs and requirements are not considered when companies evaluate and select technology. These requirements need to be included in the technology vetting process up front. For example, if a financial services company selects a collaboration site, it will need to know if any of the users are subject to the broker dealer regulations and if the technology can store such information in compliance with the requirements.

Protect Property Rights

Companies need to have policies in place about ownership of work product that is collaboratively created both with employees and third parties. Collaboration tools create a unique challenge with ownership rights. Executives should address this proactively.

Access Controls

Macro Access

Organizations need to determine what business units will be sanctioned to use a specific collaboration or social site. Someone on the executive team needs to take ownership of this type of decision as it should not be delegated down to an IT mid-level management position.

Micro Access

Determining which employees should have access to certain content and establishing the rules of the road of the collaboration and social site needs to be addressed by policy. For example, does an employee have the privileges to give a third party access to a site or file?

Discovery in Collaboration and Communication Environments

Any potentially relevant information including content created in collaboration, communication, and internal social sites may be discoverable. Each technology has unique technical realities that make discovery more or less challenging.

Before allowing use of any such technology, the lawyers need to understand the good, the bad, and the ugly to understand what discovery may look like and prepare.

When looking at the technical realities of the environment that you are considering implementing, determine if and how discovery will be impacted and conducted by company insiders when litigation hits. And for certain environments implementation decisions and technical realities will significantly impact the discovery process and the litigation. For example, certain collaboration environments may allow 100 different versions of the same

---

Be careful with basic data sources. Email, text messages, mobile data, and difficult to access data are those most often spoliated.[3]

document. Alternatively, that same technology can be configured to limit the number of versions saved to a relatively small amount. The time, expense, and risk associated with those decisions are not inconsequential.

> Digital collaboration technologies are accelerating productivity in the post-phone-call workplace, but tools like Yammer, Workplace by Facebook, and Slack have their dark side. While these channels can help speed group decision-making, they also serve as an enterprise blind spot for insider threats to do their worst—not to mention being open conduits for spreading negativity and toxic behaviors among the ranks.[4]

---

3. Judges Survey 2019, Exterro, https://judicialstudies.duke.edu/wp-content/uploads/2019/04/Judges_Survey_2019.pdf.

4. Erica Chichowski, *Insider Dangers Are Hiding in Collaboration Tools*, Dark Reading (Jun. 26, 2018), https://www.darkreading.com/vulnerabilities---threats/insider-threats/insider-dangers-are-hiding-in-collaboration-tools/d/d-id/1332155.

Rule 19

Bring Your Own Device

Executive Takeaway

Letting employees use their own technology may make business sense, but beware.

Background

Historically, companies were loath to allow their employees to use their personal computers for work for a myriad of reasons. Concerns over loss of company information, privacy issues, doing discovery on an employee personal device are just a few of the many such issues. Within the last decade the thinking has evolved regarding employees using personal devices for work. The bring your own device (BYOD) movement has institutionalized the use of personal devices at work to allow employees to use the devices they are most familiar with to get work done, with the company saving on expenses related to technologies acquisition. The transformation and thinking relates to accommodating a younger workforce that prefers to work in their technology and the realization that properly building BYOD programs can make economic sense for the company.

Business Implications

Accommodating the Workforce

While some companies have prohibited such conduct, other companies have entertained and embraced the use of such devices to do work. There are numerous implications to embracing a BYOD mindset, including attracting and retaining a more technically savvy workforce, limiting expense associated with buying and maintaining the newest technology, accommodating an expanding workforce that works remotely, and satisfying the employees' desire to work in their own technology. Additionally, BYOD tends to enhance productivity because employees can work when they are not in an office setting and because they are most comfortable functioning in their own technology.

Ownership and Use

When company information is located on a personal device it may create an issue for the company going forward. Can the company assert that it owns the information? Can the company force the employee to delete the information and/or provide the information back to the company whenever the company desires?

Security

Because BYOD devices are necessarily employee-owned technology, the company has a more challenging time properly securing their information and the device on which it sits. Various technologies have been developed to address segregation of company information on personal devices. Policy and technology professionals need to address security before employees are allowed to use their own devices for work.

Loss of Device

Because BYOD devices tend to be portable or mobile, such technology is more likely to be misplaced or lost. Companies need to preemptively protect their information by requiring software placed on the device to protect and kill the information if the device is lost or stolen. Such technologies are essential for protecting the company's interest.

Let's take a second to look at some interesting stats relevant to the BYOD market:

- The BYOD market is on course to hit almost $367 billion by 2022, up from just $30 billion in 2014.[1]
- 60 percent of workers overall use a smartphone for work purposes while 31 percent desire one.[2]
- 61 percent of Gen Y and 50 percent of 30+ workers believe the tech tools they use in their personal lives are more effective and productive than those used in their work life.[3]
- Companies favoring BYOD make an annual saving of $350 per year, per employee.[4]
- Using portable devices for work tasks saves employees 58 minutes per day while increasing productivity by 34 percent.[5]

---

1. Anna Johansson, *Growth of BYOD Proves It's No Longer an Optional Strategy*, BetaNews (2017), https://betanews.com/2017/05/12/growth-of-byod-proves-its-no-longer-an-optional-strategy/.

2. Earl Bless, Michael Alanson, and Chelsey Noble, *Consumerization: What is in Store for IT?*, Dell (July 2010), http://i.dell.com/sites/content/business/solutions/whitepapers/it/Documents/intel-imr-consumerization-wp_it.pdf.

3. *Id.*

4. *3 Big Risks of BYOD*, DMS Technology (Oct. 12, 2017), https://www.dmstechnology.com/3-big-risks-of-byod/.

5. Melanie Turek, *Employees Say Smartphones Boost Productivity by 34 Percent*, Frost & Sullivan (Aug. 3, 2016), https://insights.samsung.com/2016/08/03/employees-say-smartphones-boost-productivity-by-34-percent-frost-sullivan-research/.

Legal Implications

While BYOD has many benefits it also creates concerns regarding compliance, access, ownership of information, privacy, records retention, information security, and litigation response.

Good Policy and Training

With BYOD, having a policy that anticipates the various authority issues and proactively guides employees on what to do and not to do will be essential. Like any good policy, without training the policy likely will be insufficient to change behavior. In that regard, compliance methodology should be consulted to holistically address BYOD. (See Rule 12 on compliance methodology.)

Mobile data management tools should be considered to support policy directives and provide the company access and more control over the business content residing on personal devices.

Litigation Discovery

Litigation discovery can be a challenge as the device or software is the employee's but the information on the device may be the company's and may be relevant in the context of discovery.

BYOD Agreement with Employees

A written BYOD agreement should address the following, at minimum:

- The comingled or segmented nature of information on the personal device
- Company and employee rights to the information
- Expectation of privacy and security
- Device management
- Cost responsibilities

Rule 20

See the Challenge as Both Proactive and Reactive

Executive Takeaway

Expect the information universe to expand and be prepared to be proactive on certain issues and expect to react on others because that is just the way the new information-focused economy happens.

Background

Business is happening in new, exciting, and profound ways that will make the innovative companies the new winners. Information plays a role in making the innovators the new winners every time. Whether it is finding new cures, building products for half the cost, or selling pools of your information as a new source of revenue, business innovation will continue at light speed, propelled in large part by how we harness and harvest information. On the other hand, laws and regulations reminding companies that they need to comply and comport, won't be going away any time soon. Privacy and information security will continue to impact businesses and their ability to use information in various ways. Addressing the expanding universe of information-related law and regulation will continue to impact companies.

To this point, we have talked about some of the new business realities and some of the legal challenges that are taking place as your company gets transformed by information, with information, or deeply immersed in an information economy. Business will happen and should happen at the speed of light which will create legal, compliance, privacy, and governance challenges. Practically speaking, what that may mean is cleaning up messes after the fact and reacting to a less than optimal business landscape after it has evolved. In essence, some of the issues will have to be cleaned up and some of the issues can be preempted. In that regard, the information-aware lawyer can't be an obstructionist—he or she should be helping businesspeople move the business problem forward while mitigating risk and liability (refer to the Rule of Yes, Rule 18). It is way less expensive and disruptive to be proactive in addressing issues, problems, challenges to the extent possible. Below are some suggestions to make the information tasks less daunting.

Business Implications

The book to this point has gone back and forth between business, technology, legal, compliance, privacy, and variety of other issues that confound most big companies today. This Rule seeks to provide some high-level guidance for taking on these issues.

Governance and Ownership

When taking on information-related initiatives, there needs to be a governance structure established to ensure the right people are involved and that the company understands how the issue is going to be resolved. Thereafter, specific responsibility for specific tasks has to be delineated and documented so that the owner of the issue knows what he or she needs to do and by when. Taking on these issues holistically requires having experts from different backgrounds as part of the solution. But remember not to overwhelm specific business units or individuals with too many projects and initiatives as it will impact the outcome.

Build a Team

As we talked about in Rule 11, having the right professional backgrounds together helps solve these problems once and for all by getting the needed inputs up front. Bring those folks together to weigh in on the issue early to help solve the problem proactively. For most of these issues, if you don't have at least business, legal, and technical folks involved up front, it will likely be a failure.

Building a Plan

In our experience, taking on information issues is way more complex in big companies because of all the movable parts, all the technology implicated, and employees impacted. Documented plans that lay out each task, when they are getting done, who is responsible for getting them done, and the interdependency of the tasks will aid in this planning stage. Project management is super valuable to the enterprise and to getting things done as failure to have a written plan is a roadmap to failure.

Lean on Technology and Rely on the Village Only When You Have To

Once you have a plan, roll out the solution to the employees or whoever is responsible for taking action. And if you can rely on technology for the heavy lifting, do it. It would be great if you could fix the problem behind the scene and not involve employees. But when you have to rely upon employees make sure you make it super simple and not very time consuming, otherwise they likely won't be able to justify dedicating the time to get it done.

Be Proactive to Get Ahead of Issues

Every time the company implements a new technology there will be information output, and issues of control, access, and so much more. If company directives are not put in place proactively that will contribute to chaos and other issues.

As an example, a company should have a policy that dictates what steps need to be followed when a new technology is implemented or embedded in a product or service that collects or produces private information about a person. This type of policy will allow the organization to better manage private information proactively and ensure the right security protocols are governing the information.

Due to information sprawl in email and other storage environments, companies could predetermine what content belongs in each of the environments to make automatic purging of content legally viable once business needs are satisfied. For example, the company's shared drives or personal drives may be declared a non-record working and collaboration environment which allows employees to get their jobs done but doesn't require them to manage the content in the systems in accordance with laws and regulations mandating the record be retained for business processes. Any records created from that business process should not be stored in the non-record declared environments but would need to be stored elsewhere. Therefore, cleaning the environment's content could be automatic and based upon business need and can be established up front. In such a construct, employees wouldn't fear violating recordkeeping rules.

Another example that is relevant for many companies is migrating to cloud storage environments like Office 365. When moving to new environments, rules for management of the information should be established before the information is migrated and the tool implemented. When migrating to environments it is prudent not to bring the digital detritus with you. Efforts should be undertaken to purge the unnecessary dead content before moving to this new clean environment for cost, efficiency, and risk purposes.

Acknowledge That There Are Reactive Initiatives That Must Get Done

Most organizations have been retaining information for far too long and in large volumes that are not necessary to satisfy business or legal need. There are many explanations as to why this is now the reality for so many companies, but a few common ones are: information users don't know what information can be purged without violating the law, lawyers have created a "keep everything" mindset out of fear of improperly destroying evidence for lawsuits or investigations, no one has been given responsibility for purging electronic content, and some technology professionals assert that storage is cheap.

These partial truths have created an environment where mass volumes of information that should have been disposed of long ago continue to be stored and managed at an ongoing cost that is unnecessary and wasteful. This further impacts a company's risk profile.

There are no silver bullets to address the issue and make the problem go away cheaply and without risk, but there are ways to address the problem. Companies can assess the content en masse with reasonable diligence and technology, based upon age, the business unit from which the content was created, litigation docket, creators, or last access date. Assessing environments this way is not perfect but if done properly and can be defensible.

Similarly, technology analytics and classification technology can be used to assess information value and unearth private information or potential business content. Relying on these technologies to do the heavy classification lifting is not ideal as the tools are imperfect, expensive and sometimes complicated to use. Further the tools require up front policy tweaks to allow them to make decisions on your content, but still can be a powerful tool in helping to determine how to attack large volumes of information that employees don't have the time or expertise to take on.

LEGAL IMPLICATIONS

Being proactive when dealing with private information or company trade secrets makes sense in order to mitigate the risk of your information being hacked and stolen.

Establishing what content can be kept in certain storage environments makes downstream management easier and allows for more predictable end-of-life information purges without violating the law. Further, predictably purging content seeks to minimize risk and expense of litigation discovery.

Cleaning unnecessary and outdated content when migrating (moving information from one technological environment to another) tends to mitigate privacy, information security, discovery risks, and related expenses. It is important to remember that when your information is in someone else's cloud, unearthing it and extracting it may be more complex and expensive than anticipated because your company IT professionals are no longer in control of the environment.

Lawyers need to be involved in managing rules related to retention and disposition of information when implementing new technologies or seeking to cleanse old ones. IT professionals do not possess the business knowledge or legal expertise to make such decisions and should not be given such responsibility unless properly guided by both business unit and law department.

Most organizations are challenged to apply their old retention schedule to large volumes of electronic information because the rules are too numerous and too detailed to allow regular employees to know which rule to apply. Lawyers with retention expertise should seek to simplify retention rules and therefore make them easier to apply. A higher-level, "big bucket" approach (See Rule 11) also make for easier application by technology, which takes the records retention burden away from employees and automates it with the aid of technology.

With passage of the laws like GDPR and other privacy and information security regulations, it makes sense for companies to revisit their retention schedules and how long information is being kept. Some organizations take the view that retention of information should be stated as "at least x period of time." In today's environment where GDPR is mandating that companies keep information only as long as necessary and in conformity with the original intended purpose of the information, such related policies should be revisited as well.

Conclusion

Without a tool to extract and unearth patterns from terabytes of stored information, a new blockbuster product will never be born.

Without a way to connect riders with drivers, friction free, Uber doesn't exist.

Without self-learning and self-correcting robots, the warehouse would be less efficient and packages would take days longer to arrive at the customer's door.

Without a way to know that a part is malfunctioning somewhere in the thousands of miles of electricity transmission lines, a wildfire could erupt, decimating a town.

Without the ability to connect the billions of data chunks into some useable information, Noah's genetic defect is not found and addressed.

And without a leader to lead, the information universe remains an unknown, ill-managed mass of risk and lost opportunity.

For executives, officers, boards, and their advisors, including lawyers, *The Executive's Guide to Navigating the Information Universe* is a purposefully wide but shallow look at all things information impacting companies today. For the smart companies, information is their lifeblood and future. For other less-evolved companies, information can be a growing pile of headache and harm. This guide is a way for executives to seize both the desire to harness information for competitive advantage and manage the legal, risk, and compliance issues of their information trove. We hope the journey was helpful and brought to the fore how important it is for leadership to nurture an information-minded culture. During our journey we have been lots of places. Here's how we got to this place.

In Rule 1 we explored how certain business leaders were taking full advantage of the new evolving information economy and how new ways of doing business were made possible by seeing information as both a differentiator and perhaps a new lease on their company's business life. No matter what, more businesses see information as a revenue source than ever before. In Rule 2 we stressed the importance of seeing innovation as a differentiator.

In Rule 3 we explored the notion of control and reminded leaders that while most companies have lost more and more control of information over time, in many cases it was for the better. On the surface that seems unnerving. But in truth, the cloud and various third parties working on your behalf can do better at managing company information than the company can do itself. It also cautioned that lawyers are essential partners in managing relationships with anyone touching company information.

In Rule 4 we provided an overview of what data, information, and records are in order to help leaders understand that there are many different information-focused initiatives likely happening contemporaneously at most companies that they should know about. Data management is essential to have clean structured data elements to cross-pollinate business. Information governance is holistic information management from a policy, risk, legal, and compliance perspective while records management is the management of a small subset of information defined as records. All this is important for executives to contextualize what the company is using its available resources on and why. In Rule 5 we explained how and why the information universe is chaotic and how executives could help unwind the mess.

And in Rule 6 we asserted that executives were central to creating a culture that sees information as an asset requiring protection. In that regard, economic espionage or the stealing or company information costs U.S. businesses around a billion dollars per day and costs American workers millions of jobs.

In Rule 7 we explored how to monetize information while being mindful of privacy minefields and in Rule 8, we helped executives understand that information value changes over time and what can be done about it. In Rule 9 we argued that despite common misconceptions, storage for big business costs significant resources and that keeping more information for longer periods of time increases the risk profile for privacy and information security. In Rule 10 we explored the expanding legal environment impacting information in various ways and why companies should expect greater regulation of information going forward.

In Rule 11 we explored the increasingly complex world of conflicts within the organization over the various uses of information. While big data demands more information for longer periods of time, privacy laws generally mandate that companies keep less information for shorter periods of time. In Rule 12 we explained that compliance methodology is like an information mismanagement insurance policy. When things go wrong—and they always do—having a methodological approach for companies to institutionalize doing the right thing may be the difference between winning and losing big time.

In Rule 13 we explored how companies are using analytics, artificial intelligence, and machine learning software applications to answer business questions by connecting dots too plentiful for people to analyze and unearthing insights otherwise hidden from the company. And in Rule 14 we implored executives to redouble efforts to manage privacy "like your company's reputation depends on it." In Rule 15 we explored the need to create a culture of information protection to protect the company's information crown jewels.

In Rule 16 we explored how successful companies are building transparency into their Information to be "faster, better, cheaper" while also being legally compliant. In Rule 17 we talked about how the Internet of Things creates both exciting opportunities and serious risks. In Rule 18, we explored the need for leaders who tend to be risk averse to celebrate information technology to make their companies more information forward and bring in the best and brightest talent. In Rule 19 we explored how BYOD makes business sense and also promotes a happy workforce. Finally, in Rule 20 we explored the notion that some information issues were best addressed by being proactive while others would happen and have to get addressed reactively.

Information has never been more plentiful and has never moved across the globe as fast as it does now. Tomorrow there will be more information and it will move faster. There will be new technologies that create a new category of information that will present new challenges and opportunities. It is for you to make something great from this mass of information.

It is for the forward-looking executives to see the good, the bad, and the ugly of information and make it come to life for their company while mitigating any downsides. That is the challenge and opportunity. That is the accretive value of information but also its liability. Failure to embrace this new economy, where business meets risk and law meets technology is tantamount to mismanaging a corporate asset of information. And failing to see that new path likely means that tomorrow another company will be eating your lunch, drinking from your trough, and sitting on top of the world your company could have and should have owned.